France
Coloring Book

FOR KIDS 4-12

Copyright ©2021

inkHORSE
Publishing

All Rights Reserved

This Book Belongs to:

Paris

CHEF

JOYEUSE SAINT VALENTIN!

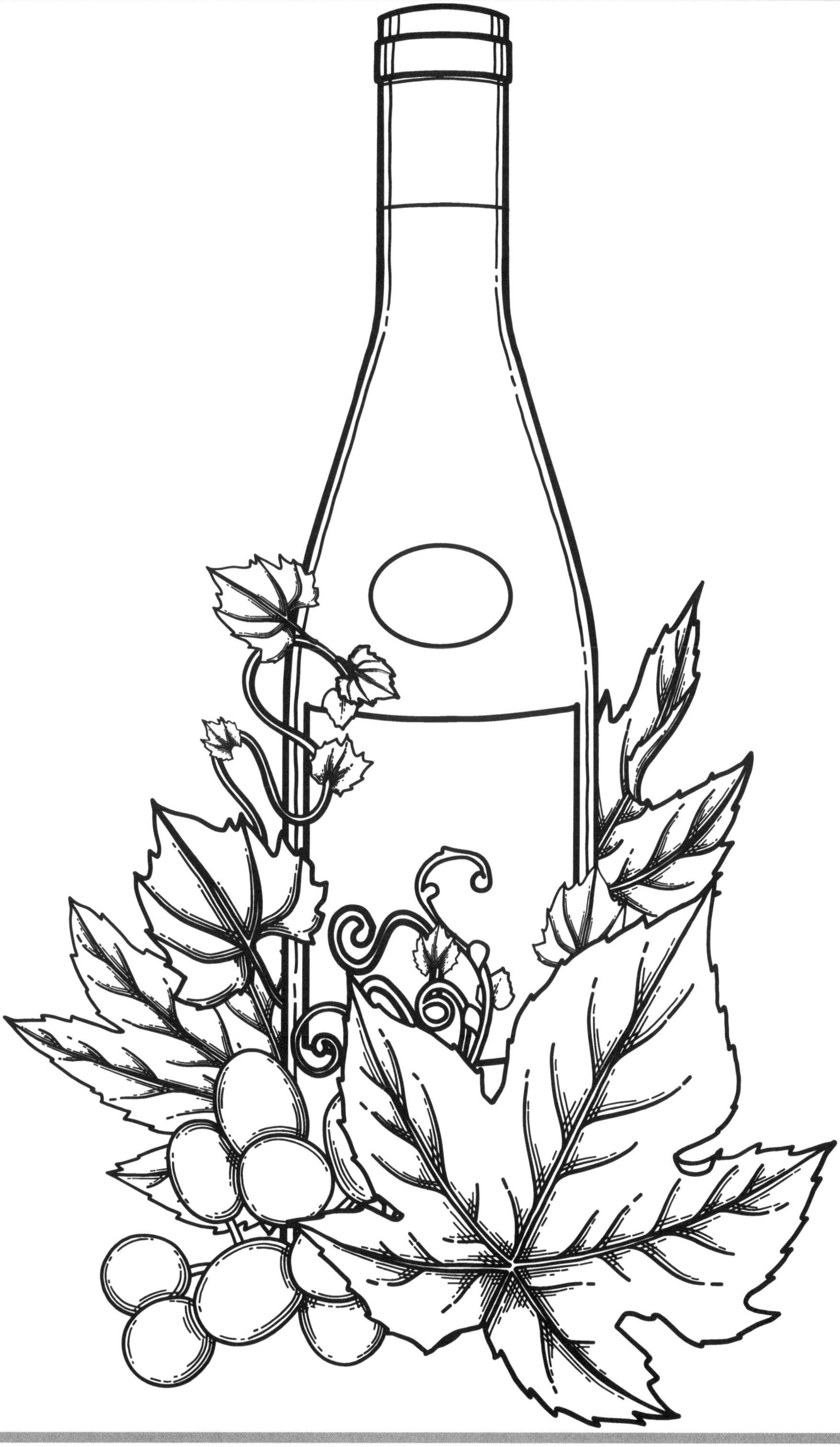

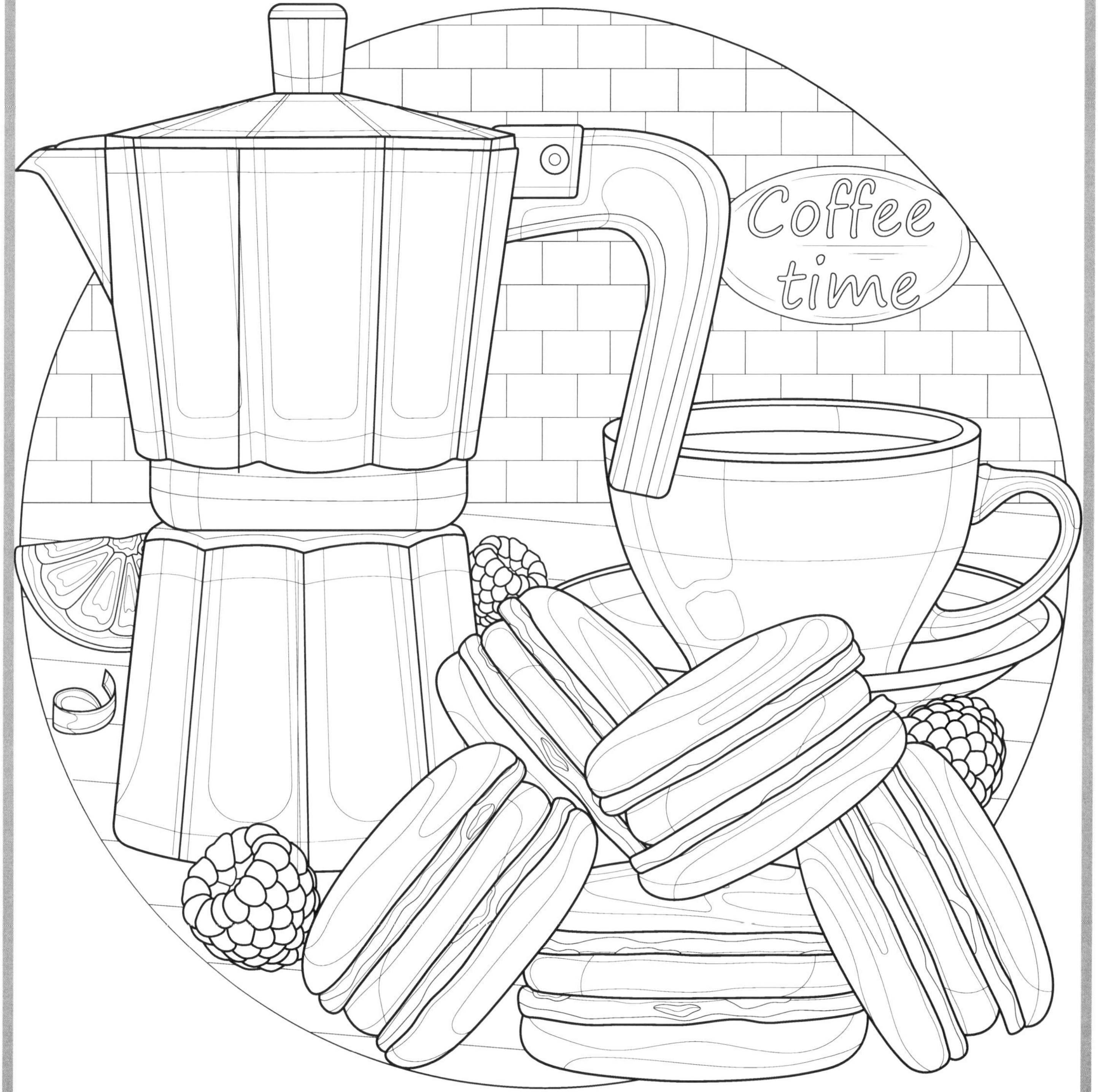
Coffee
time

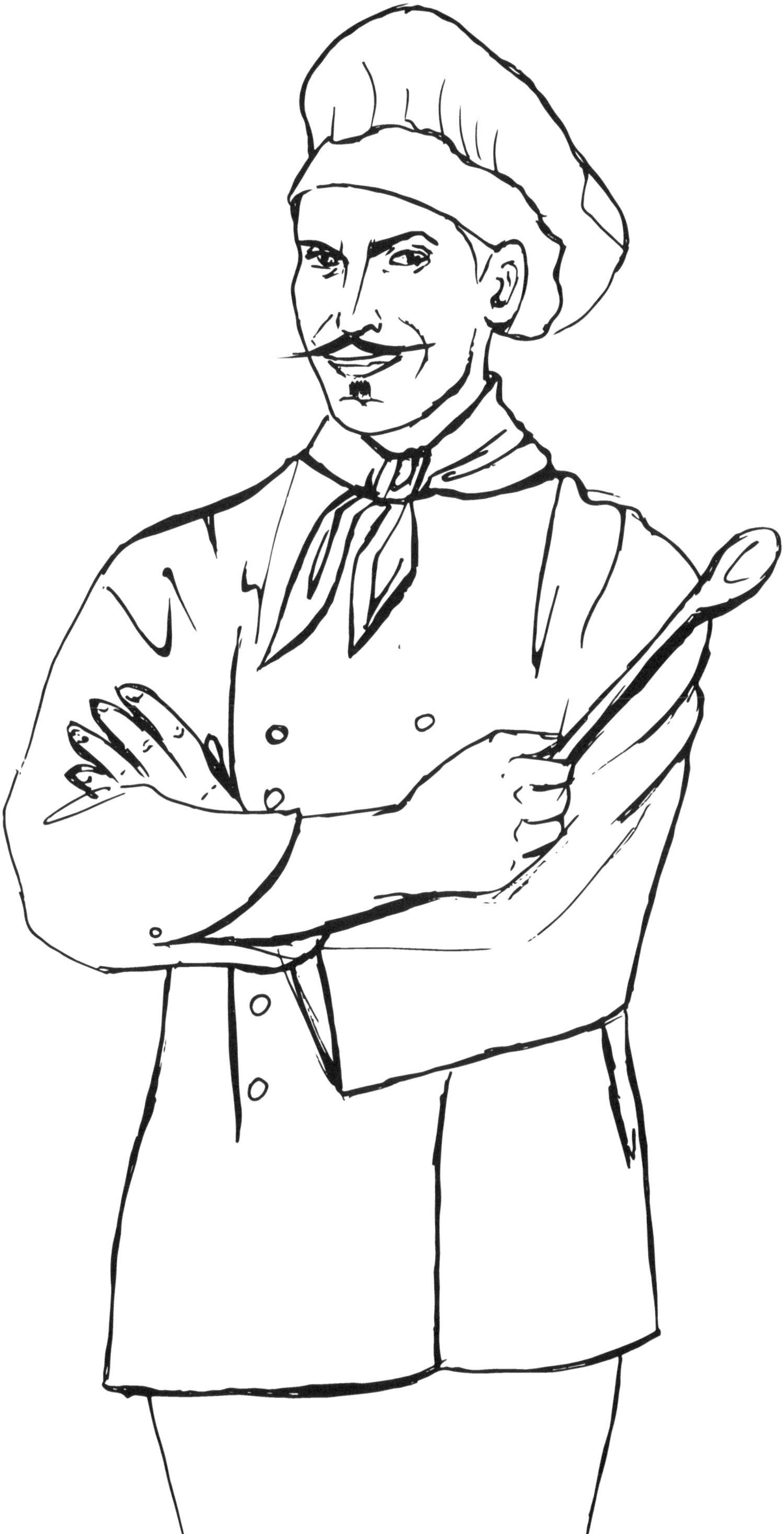

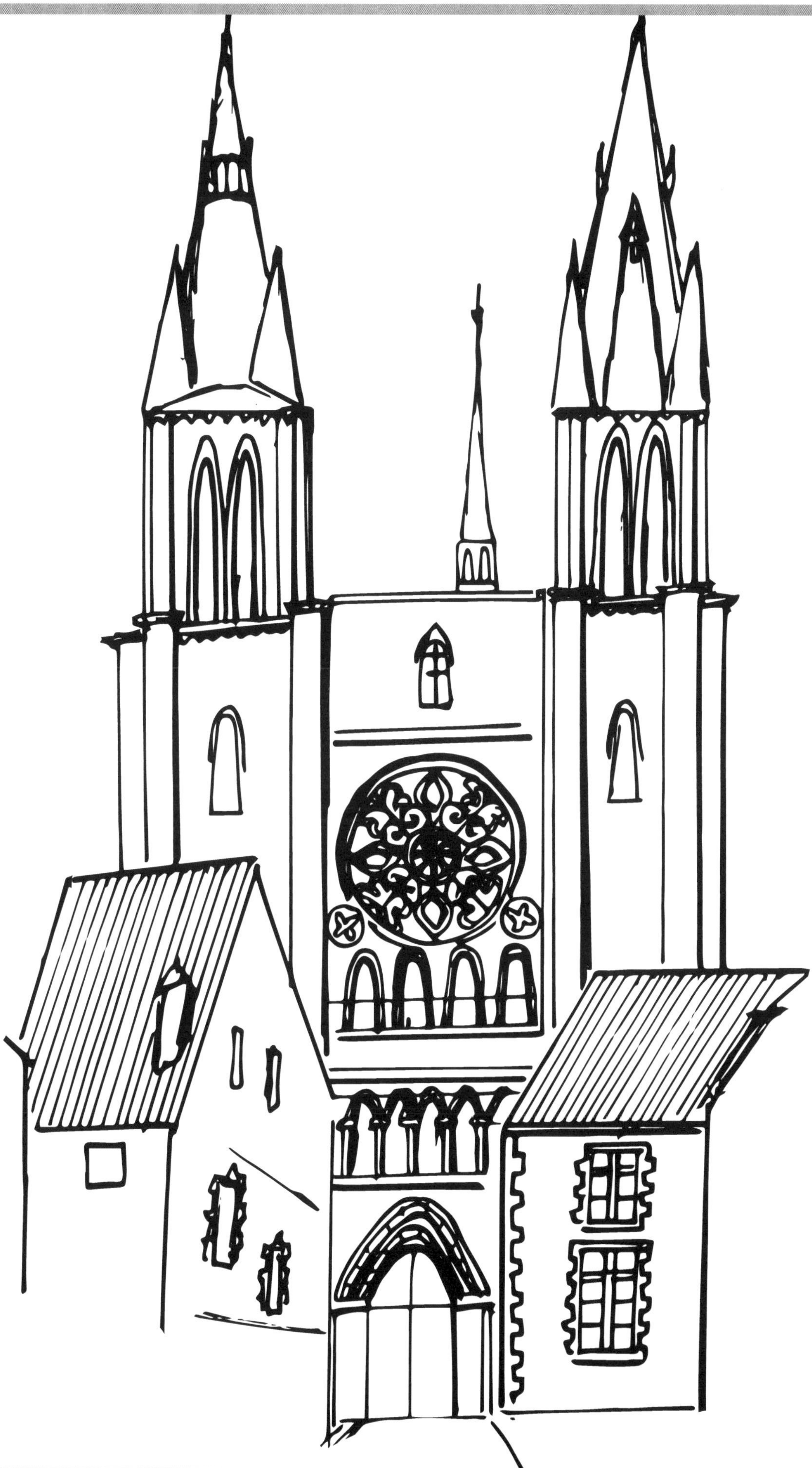

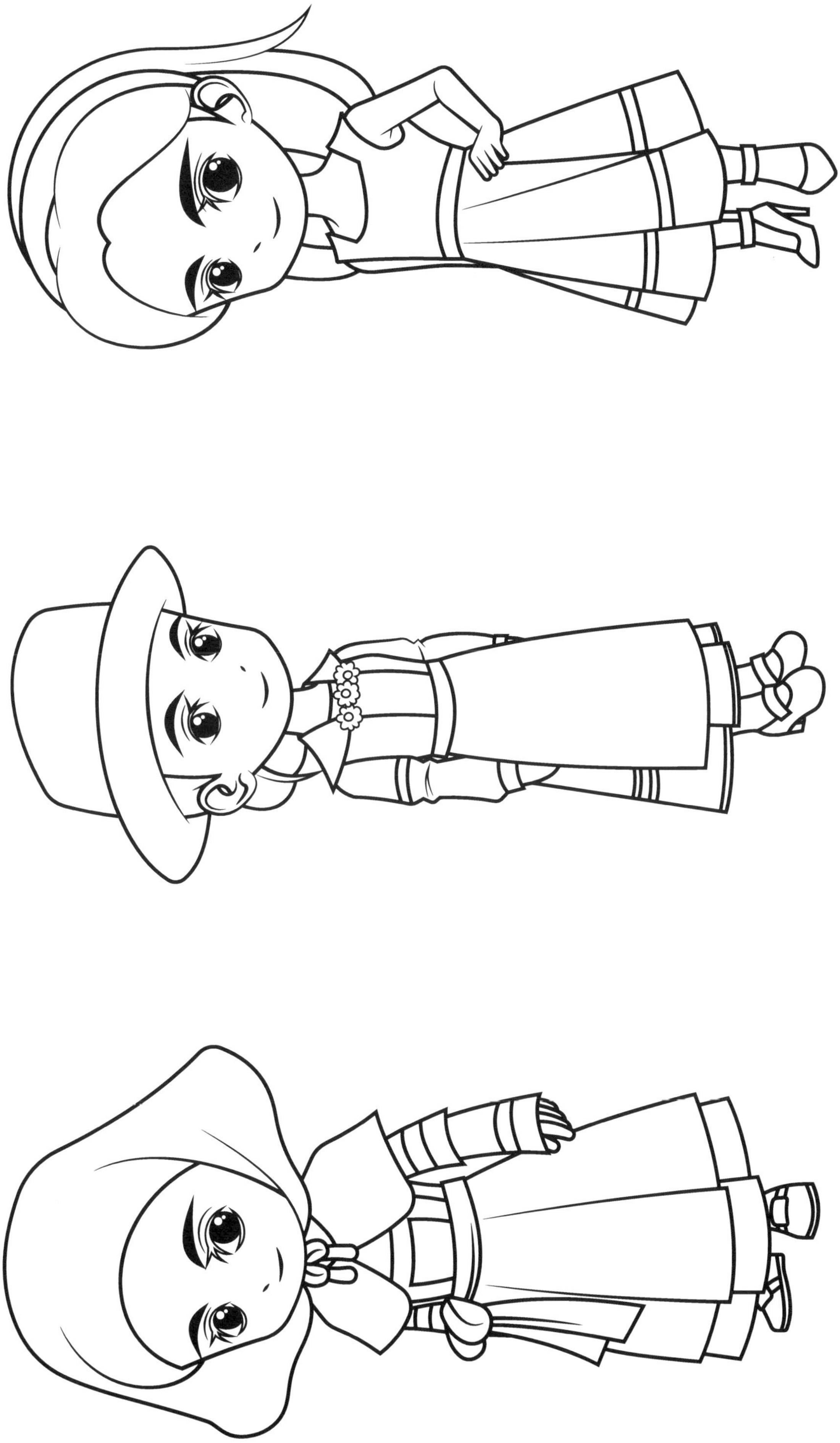

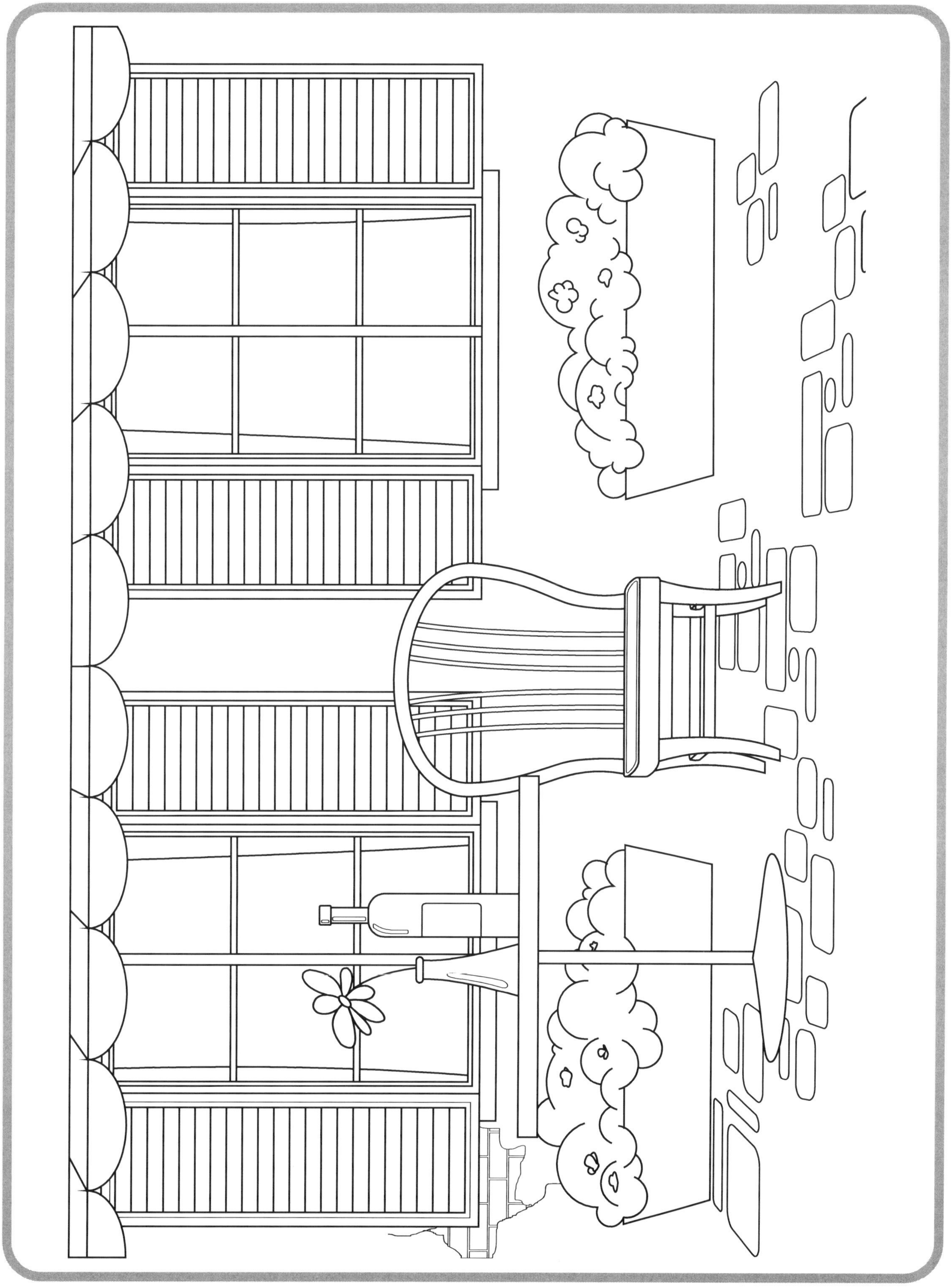

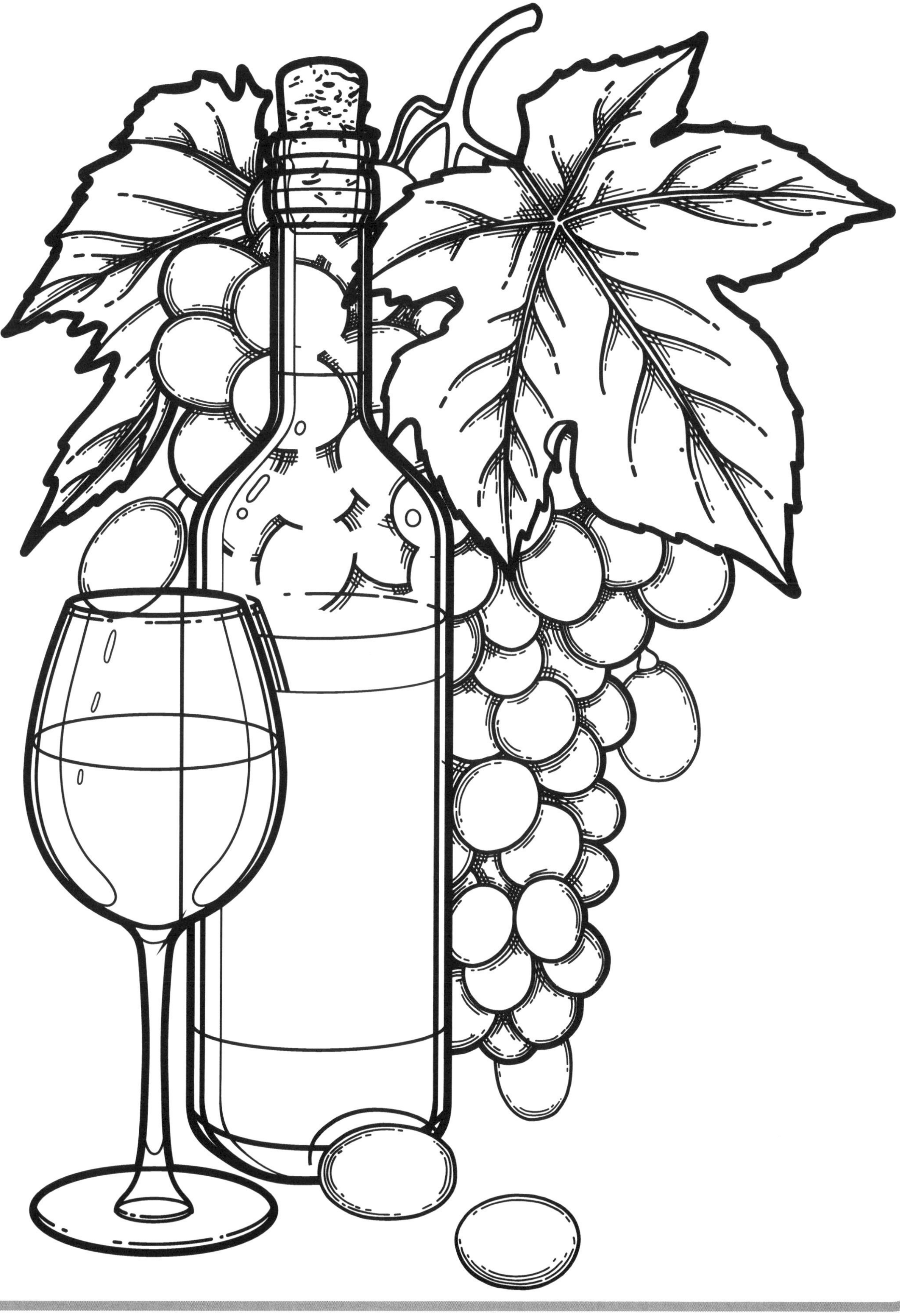

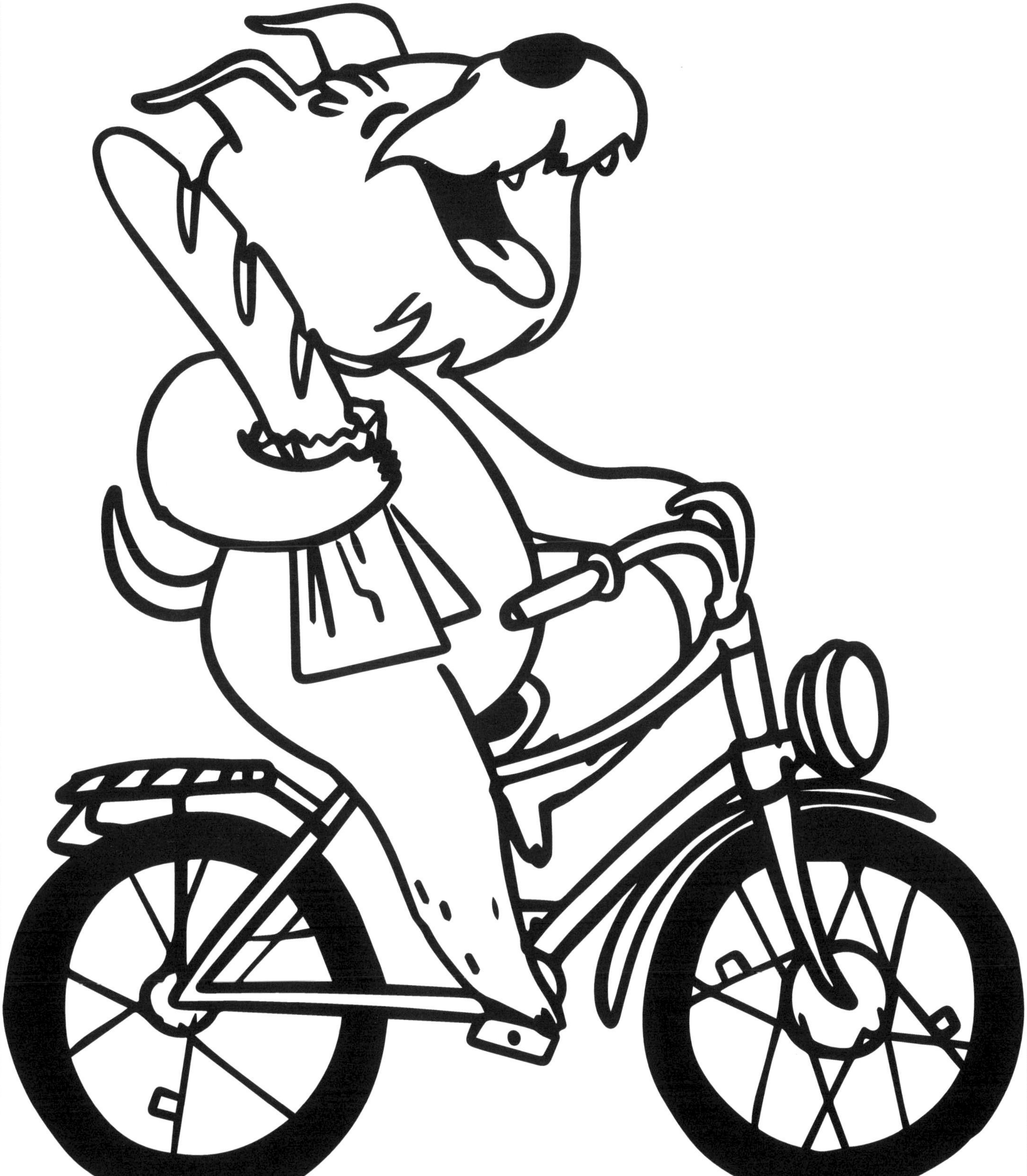

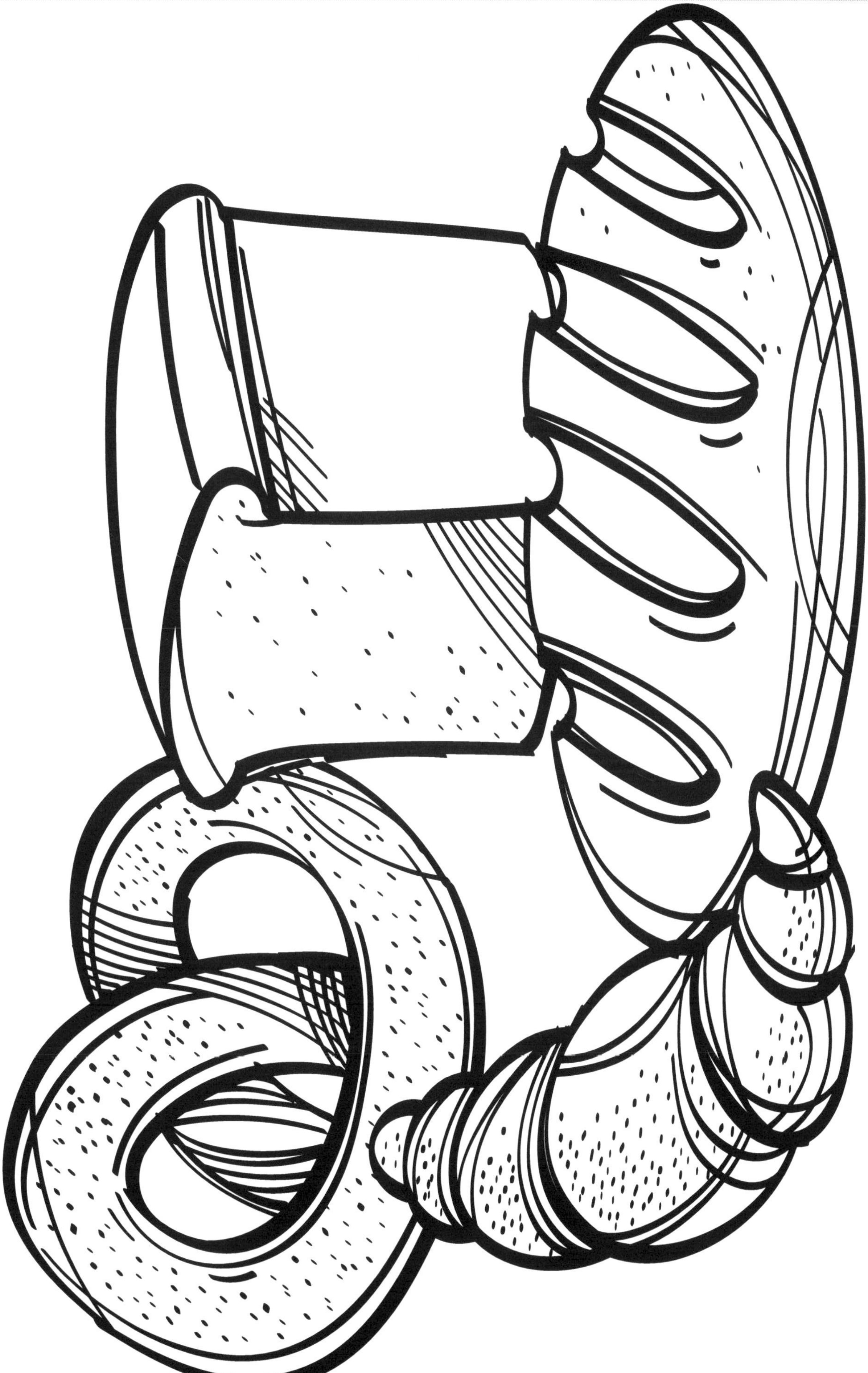

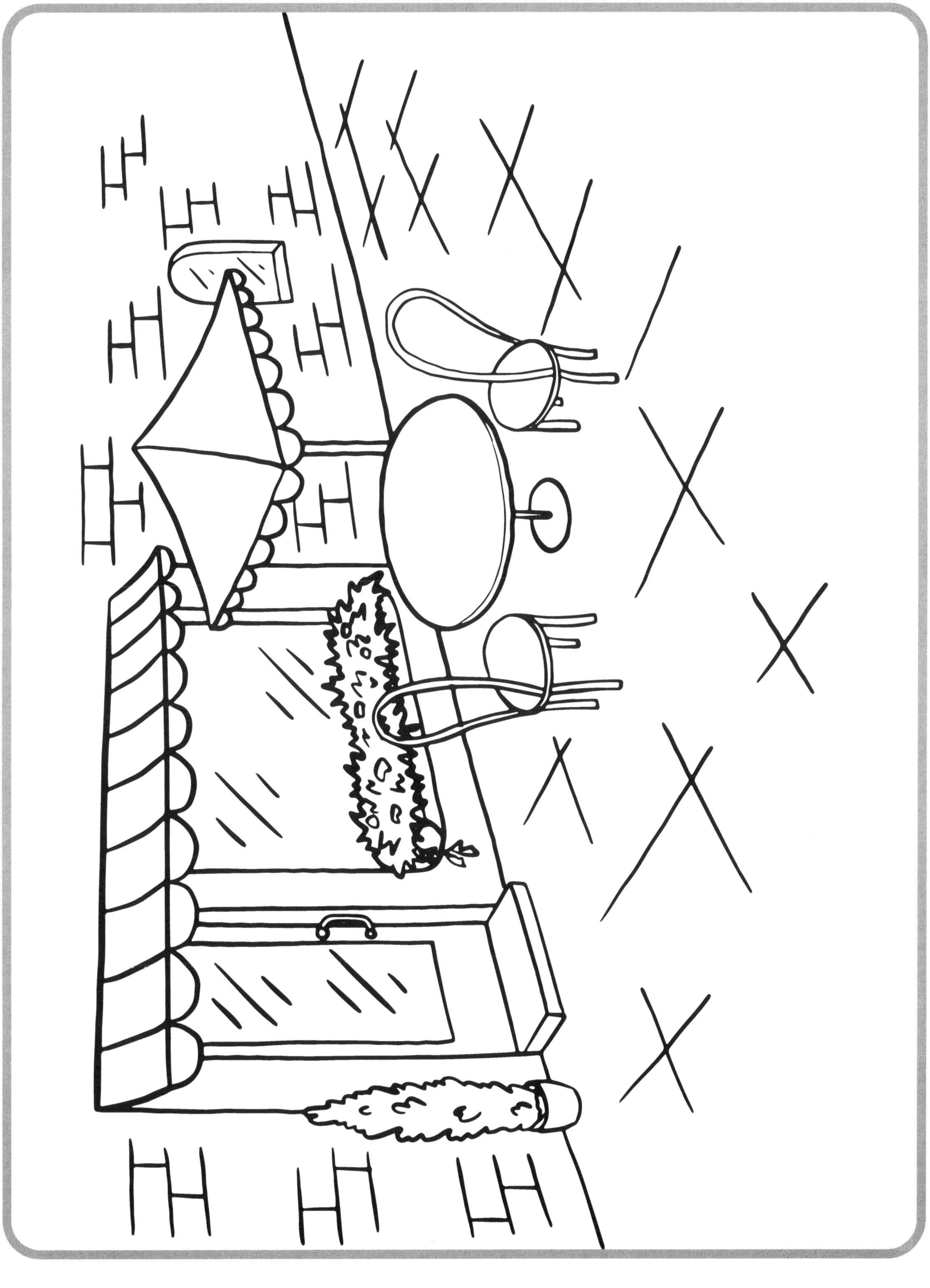

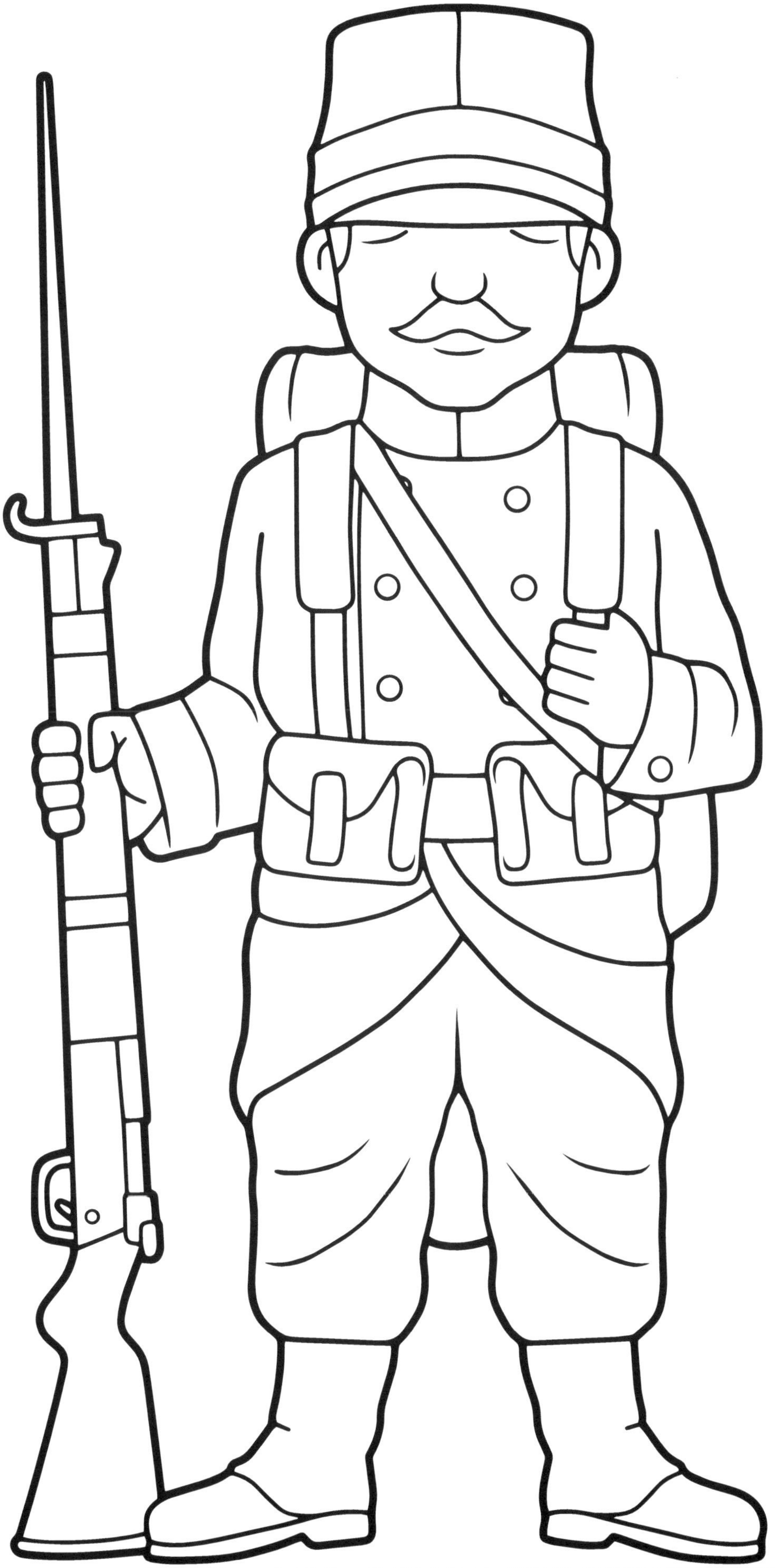

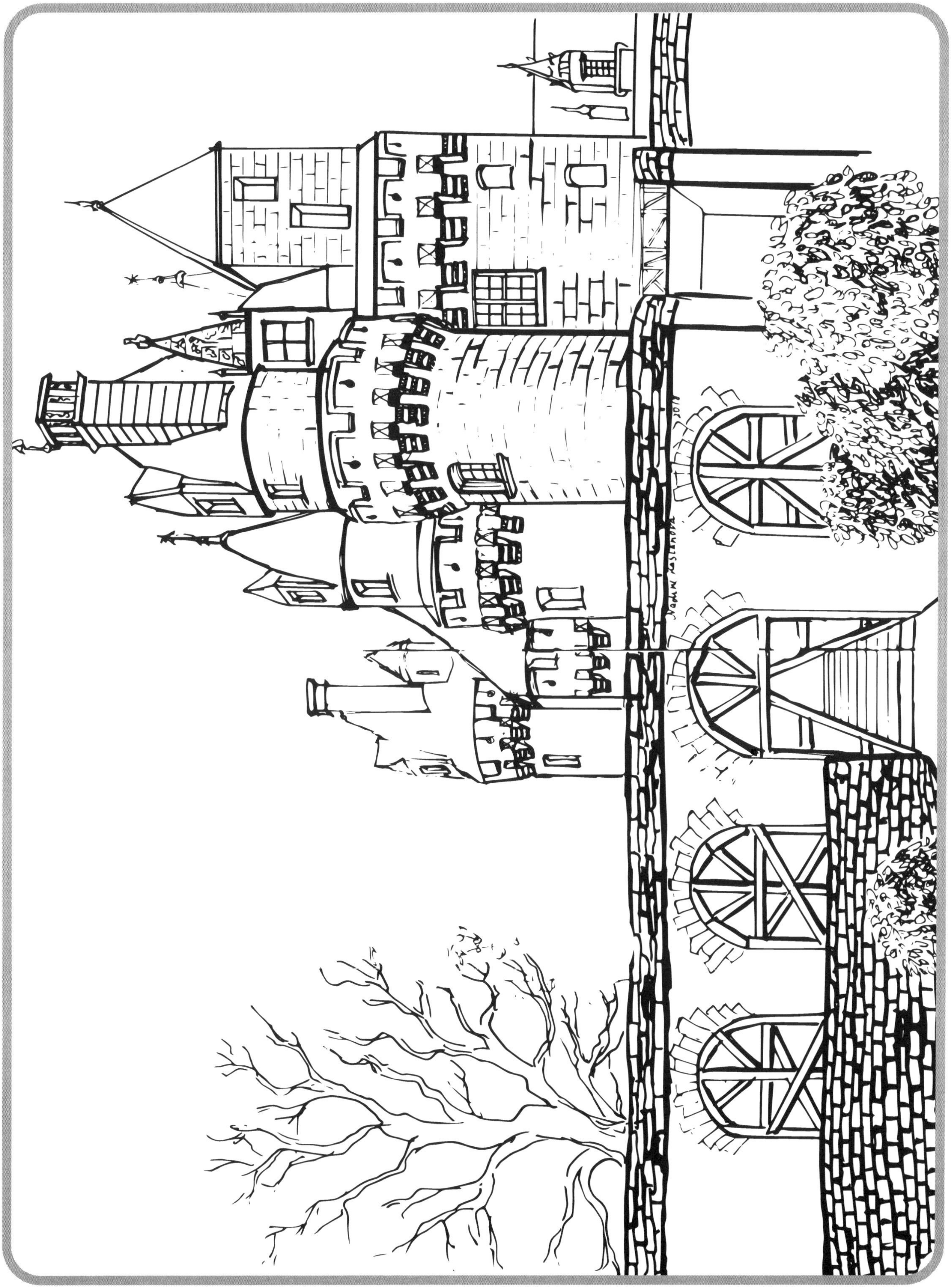

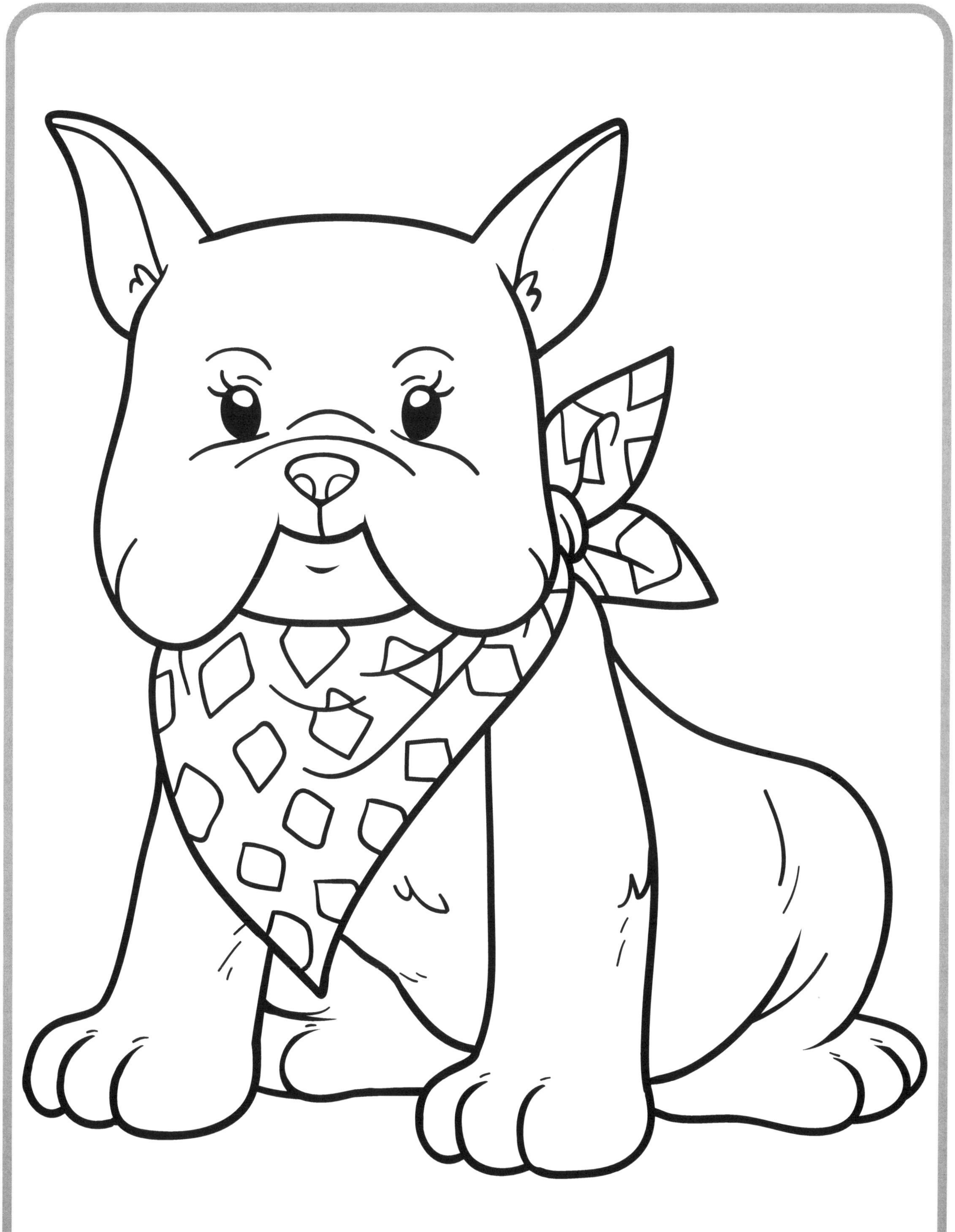

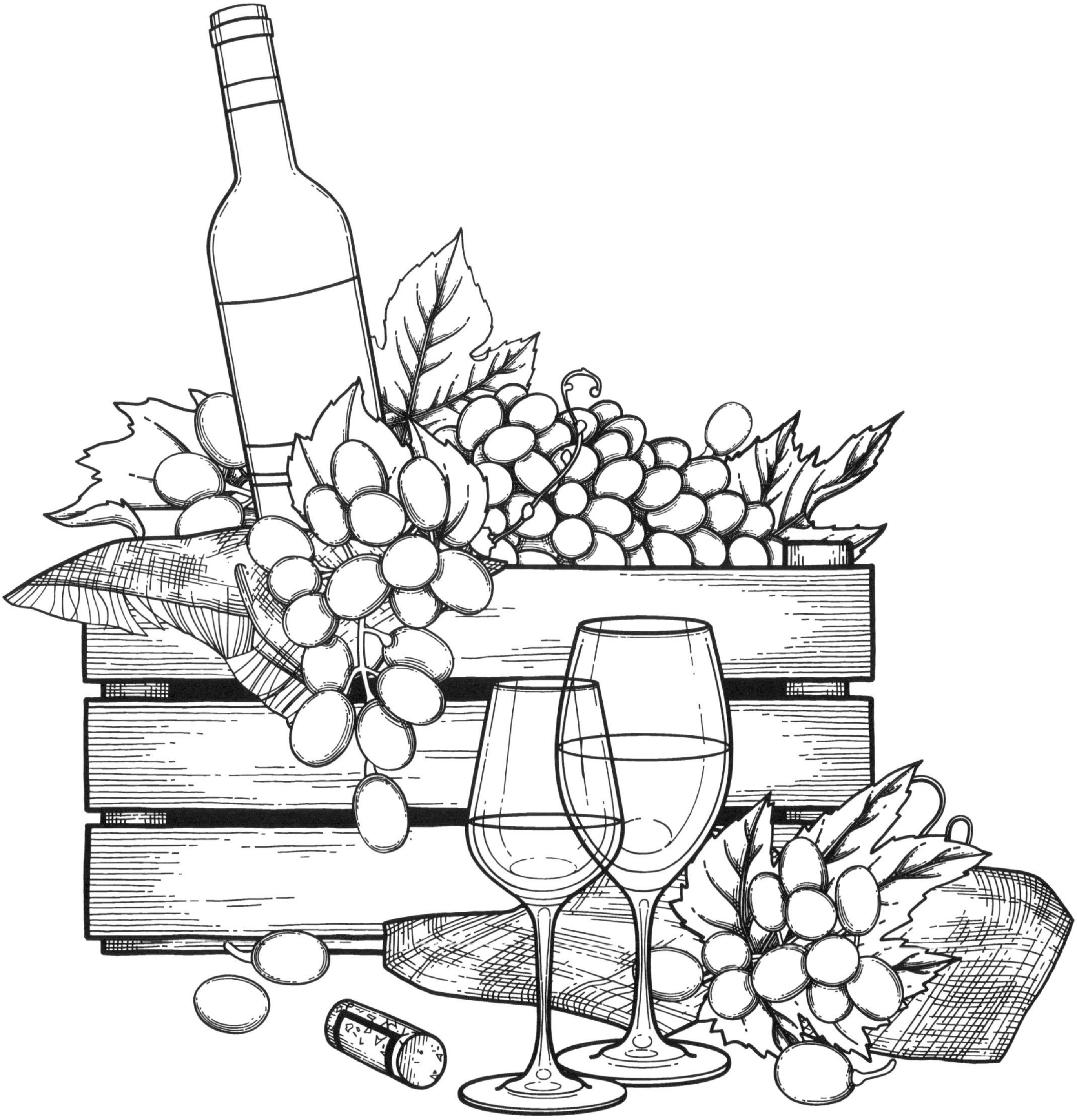

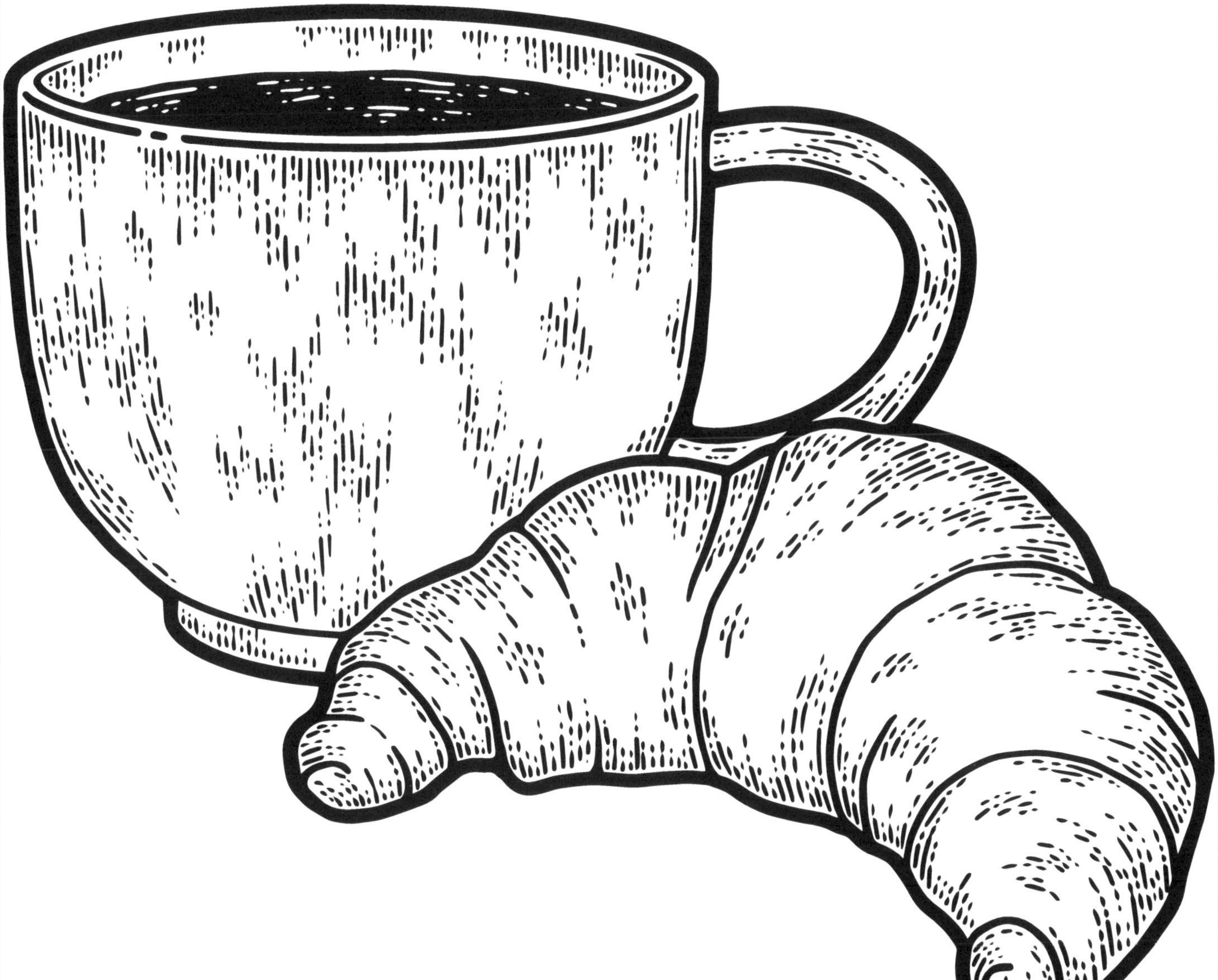

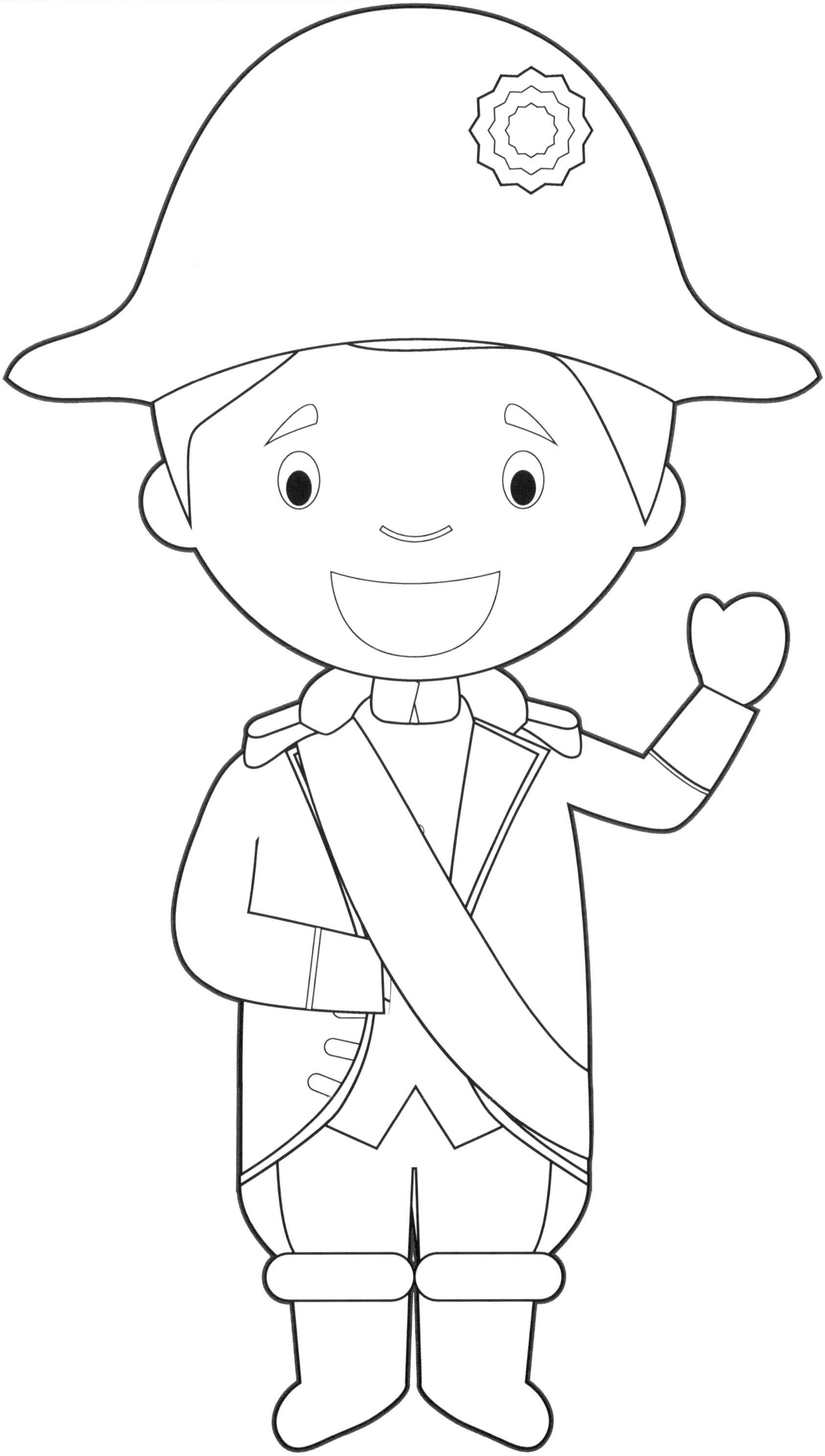

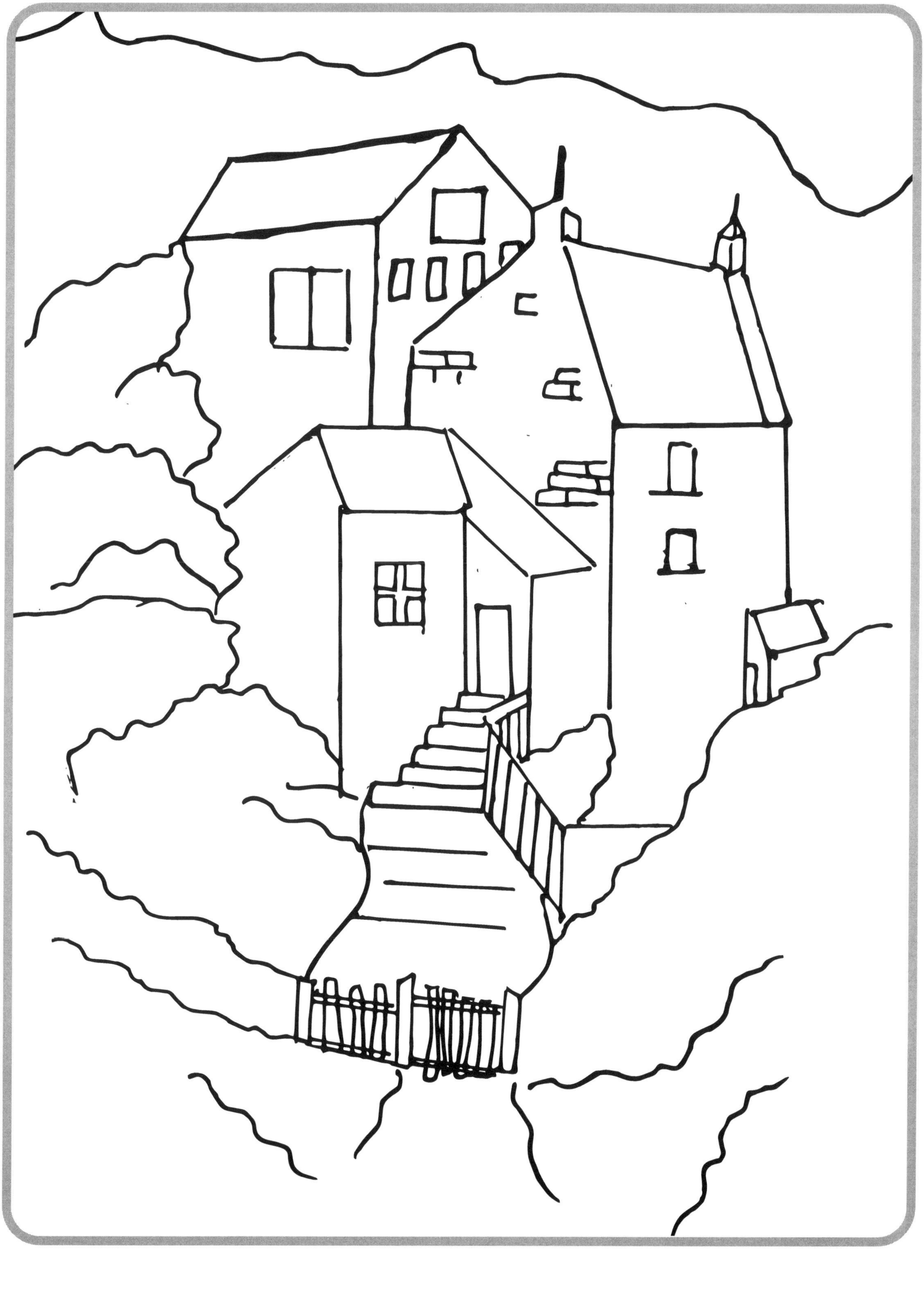

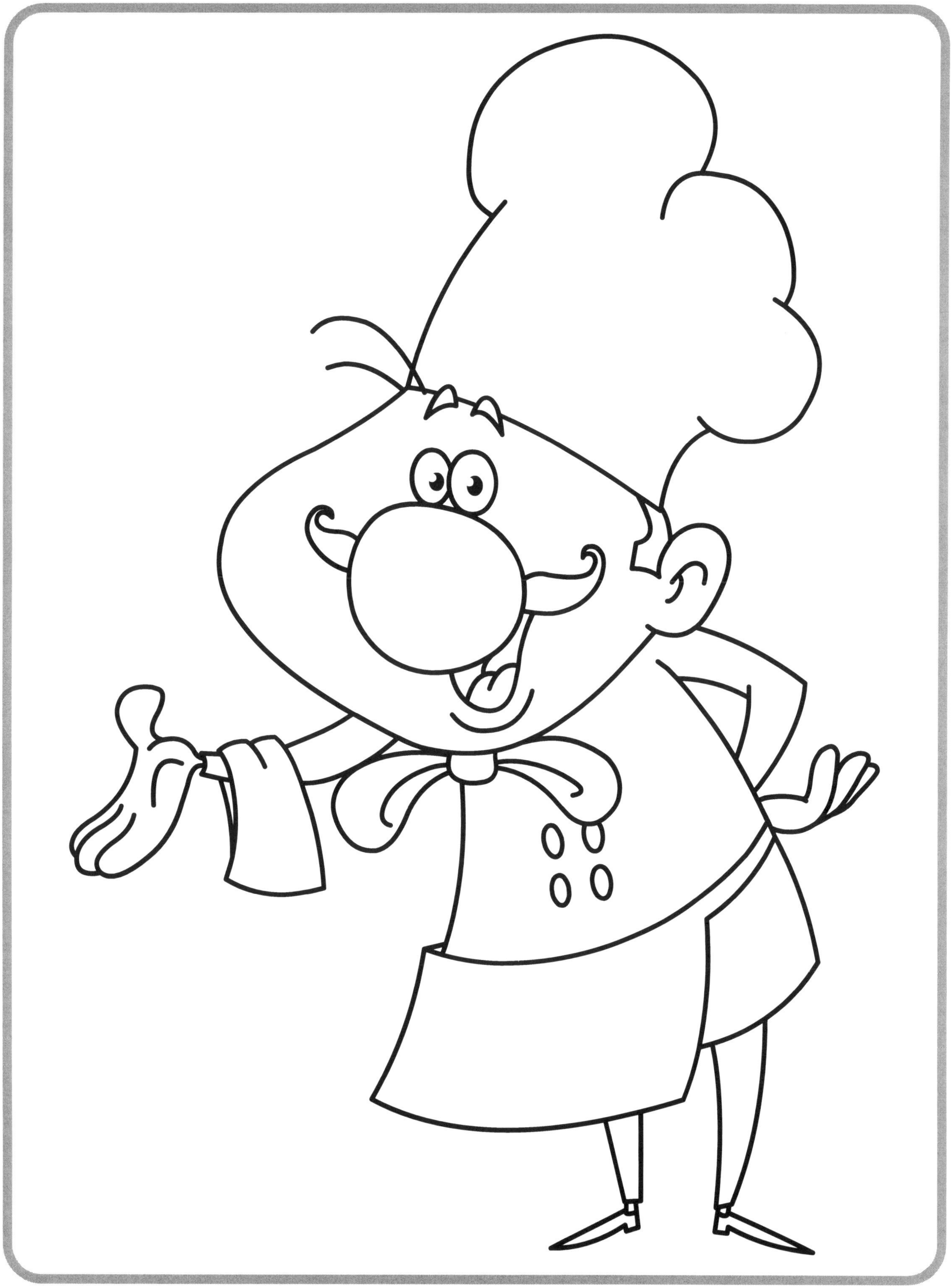

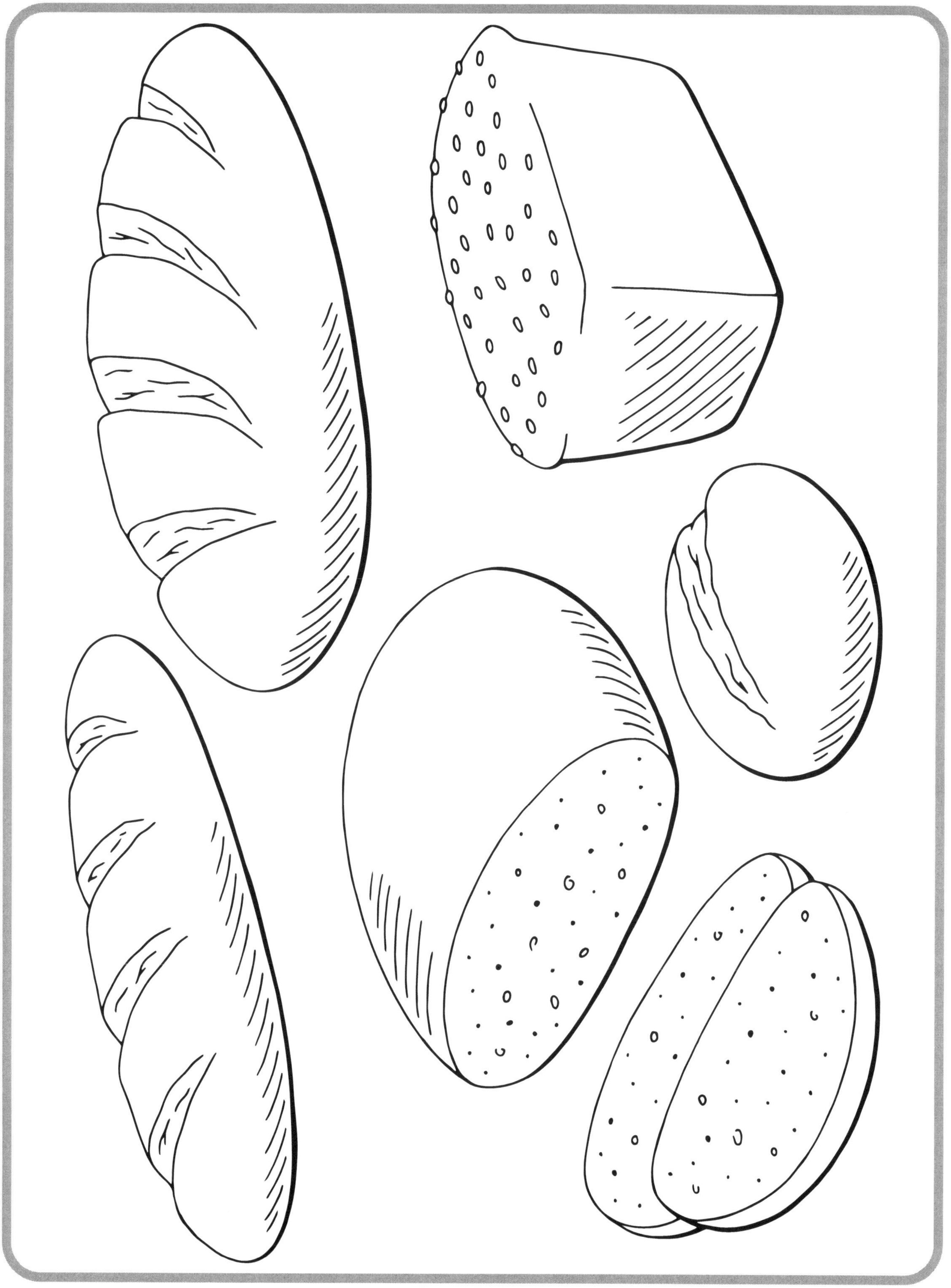

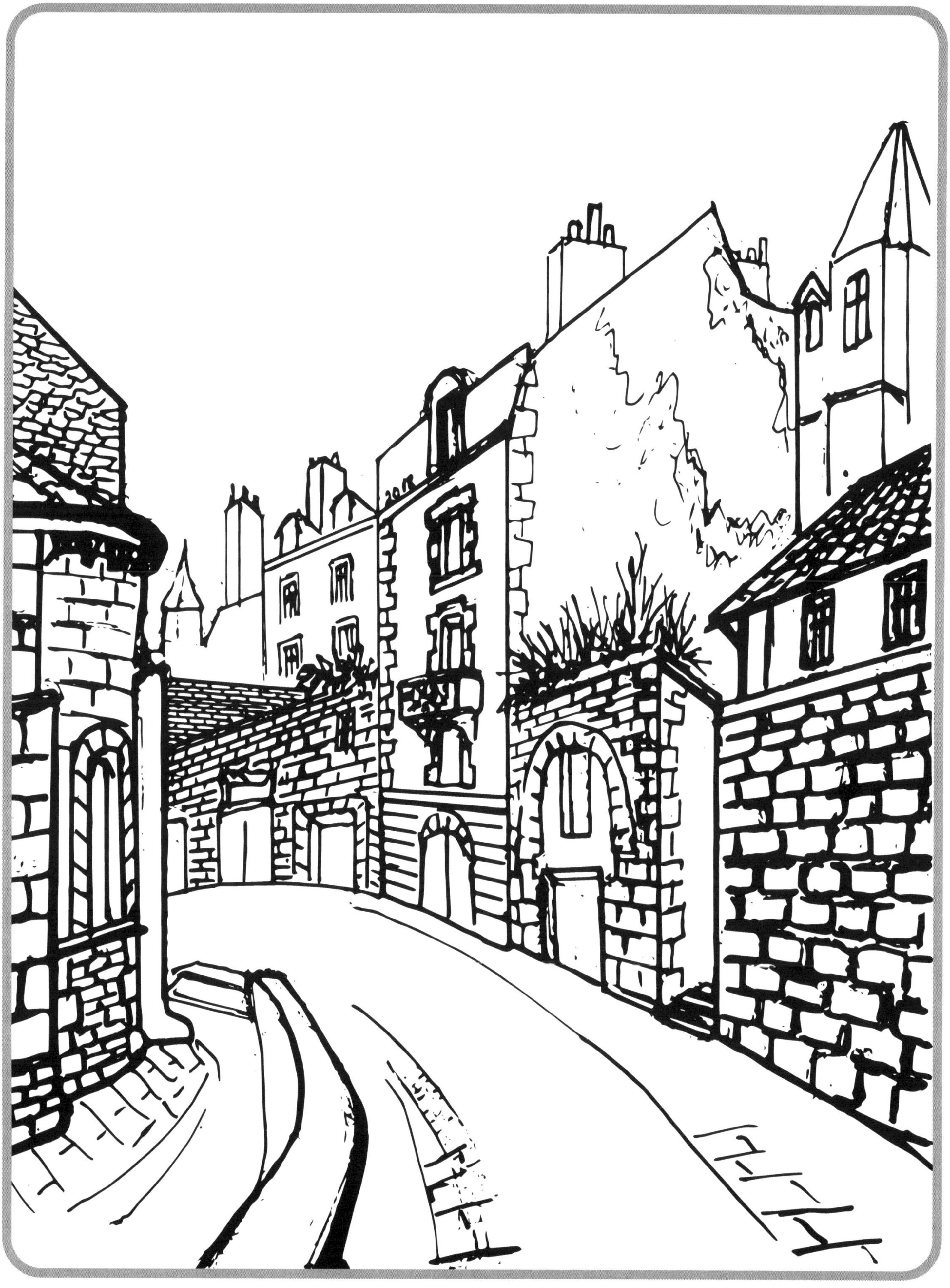

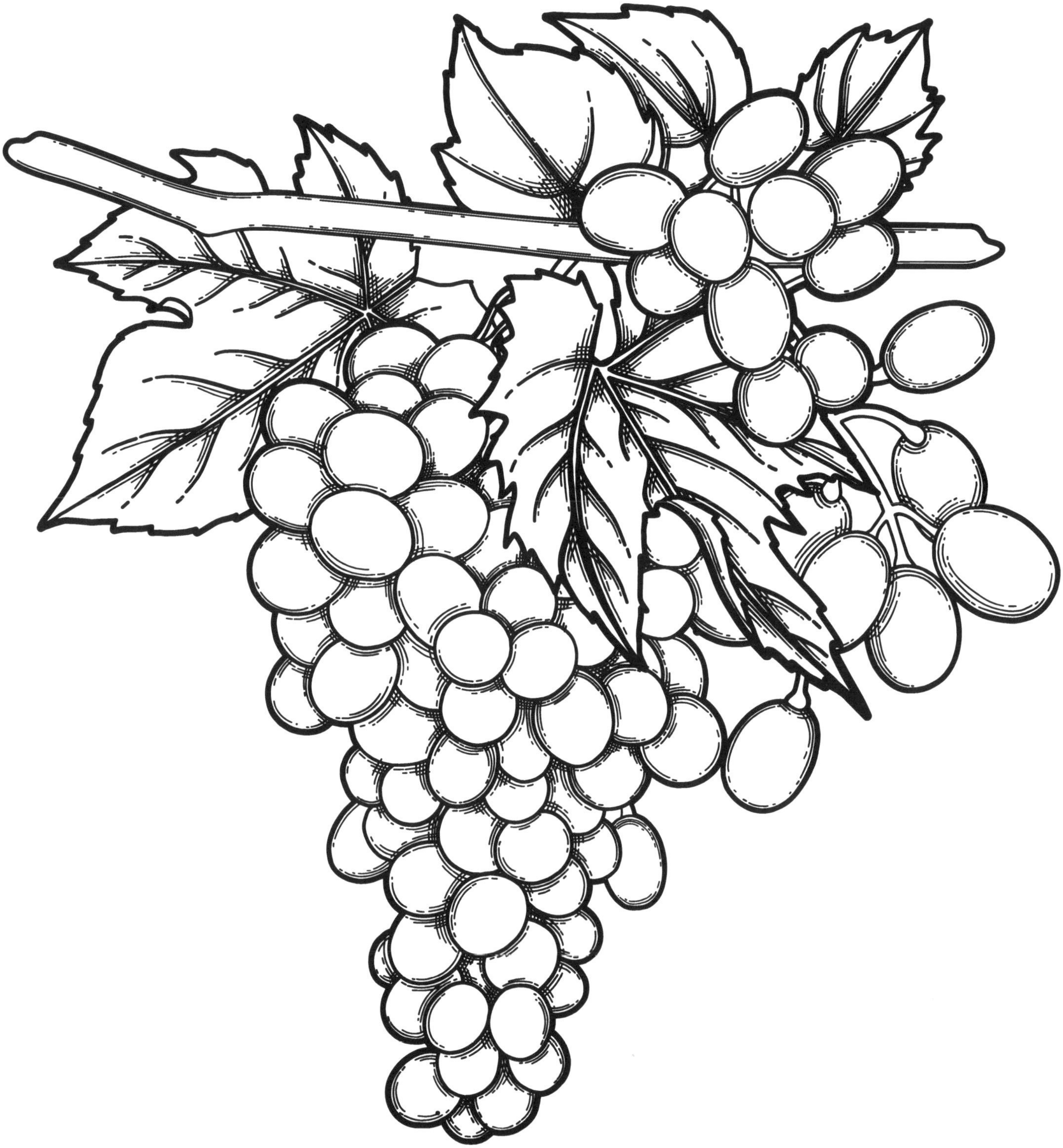

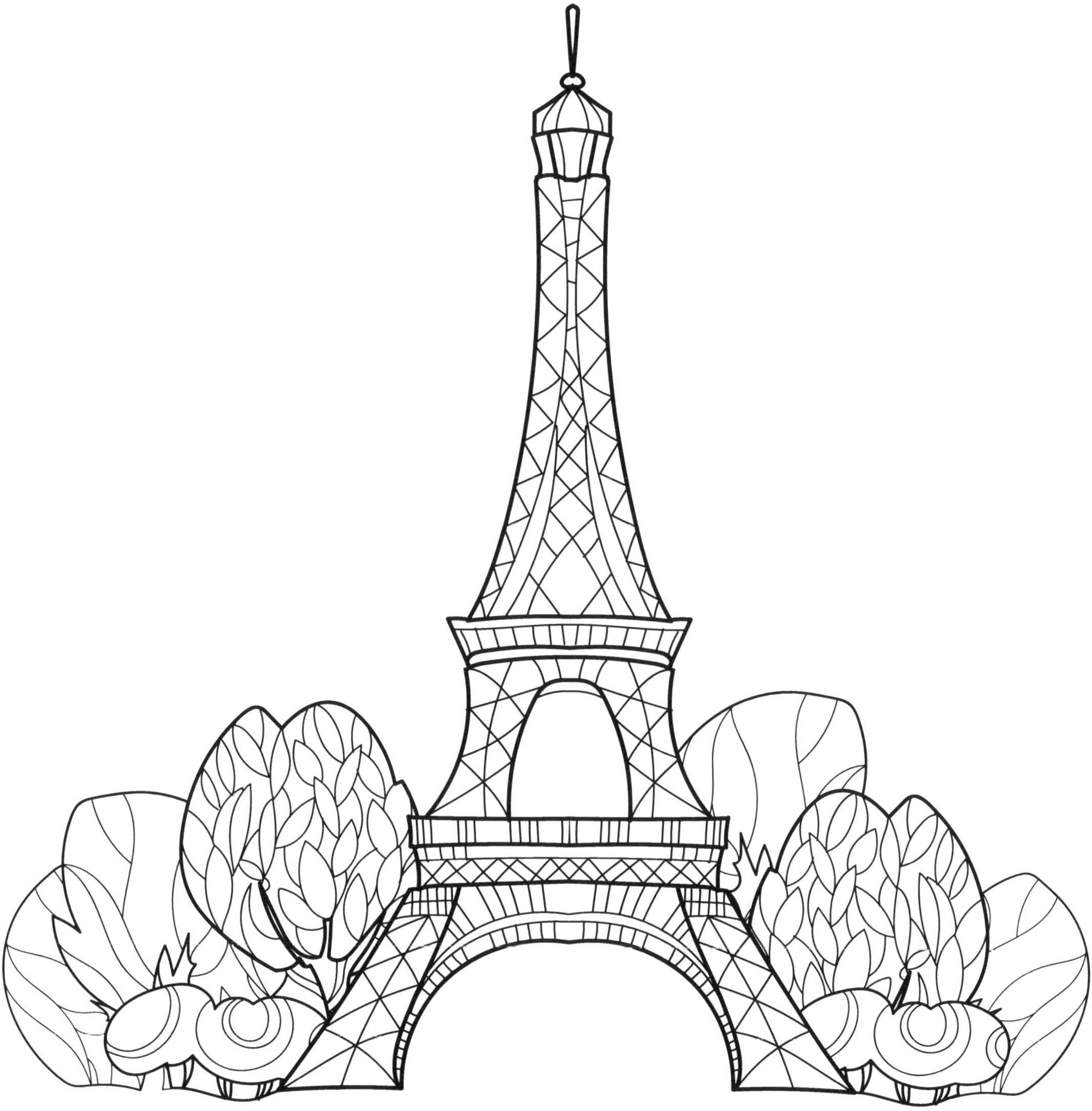

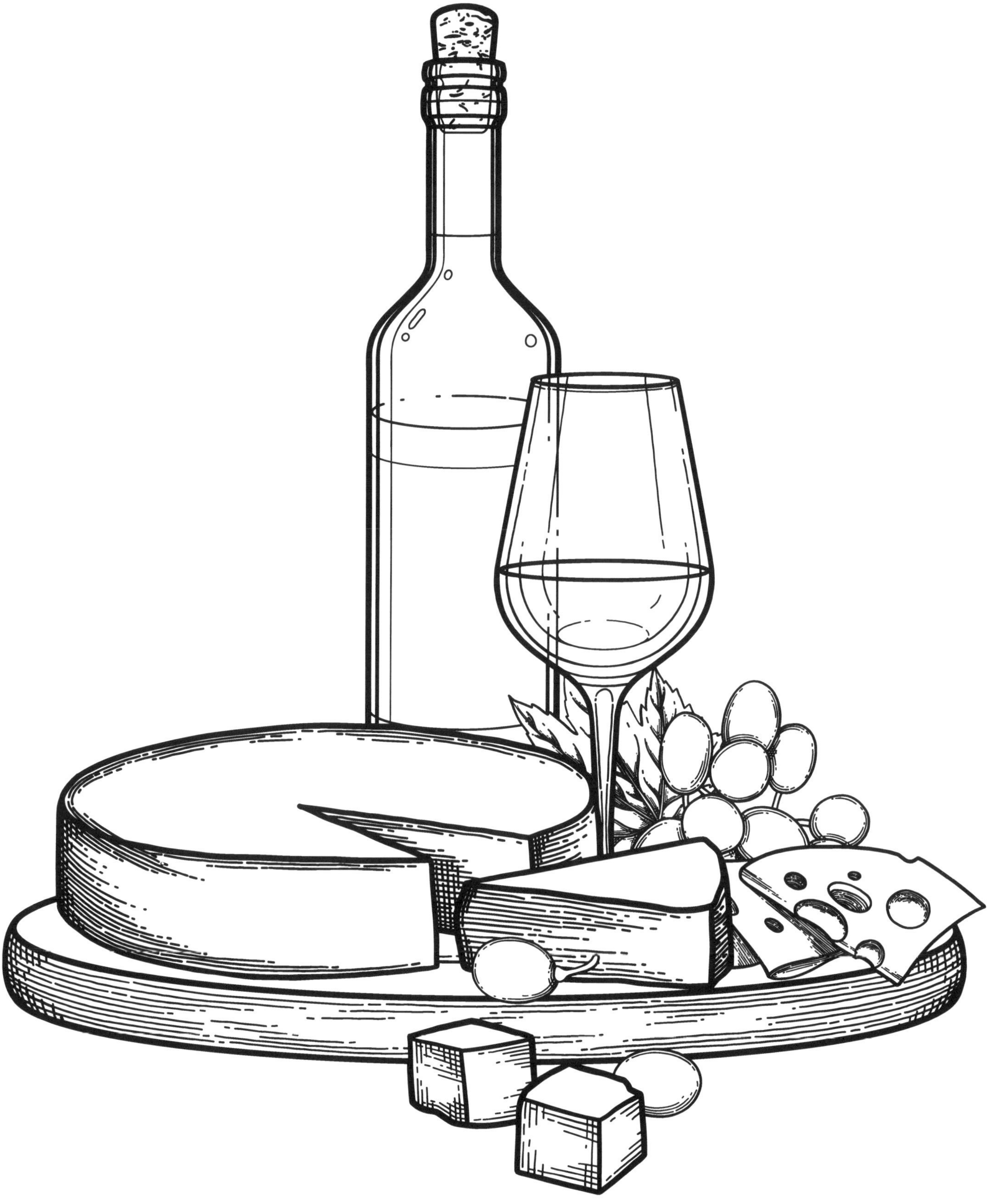

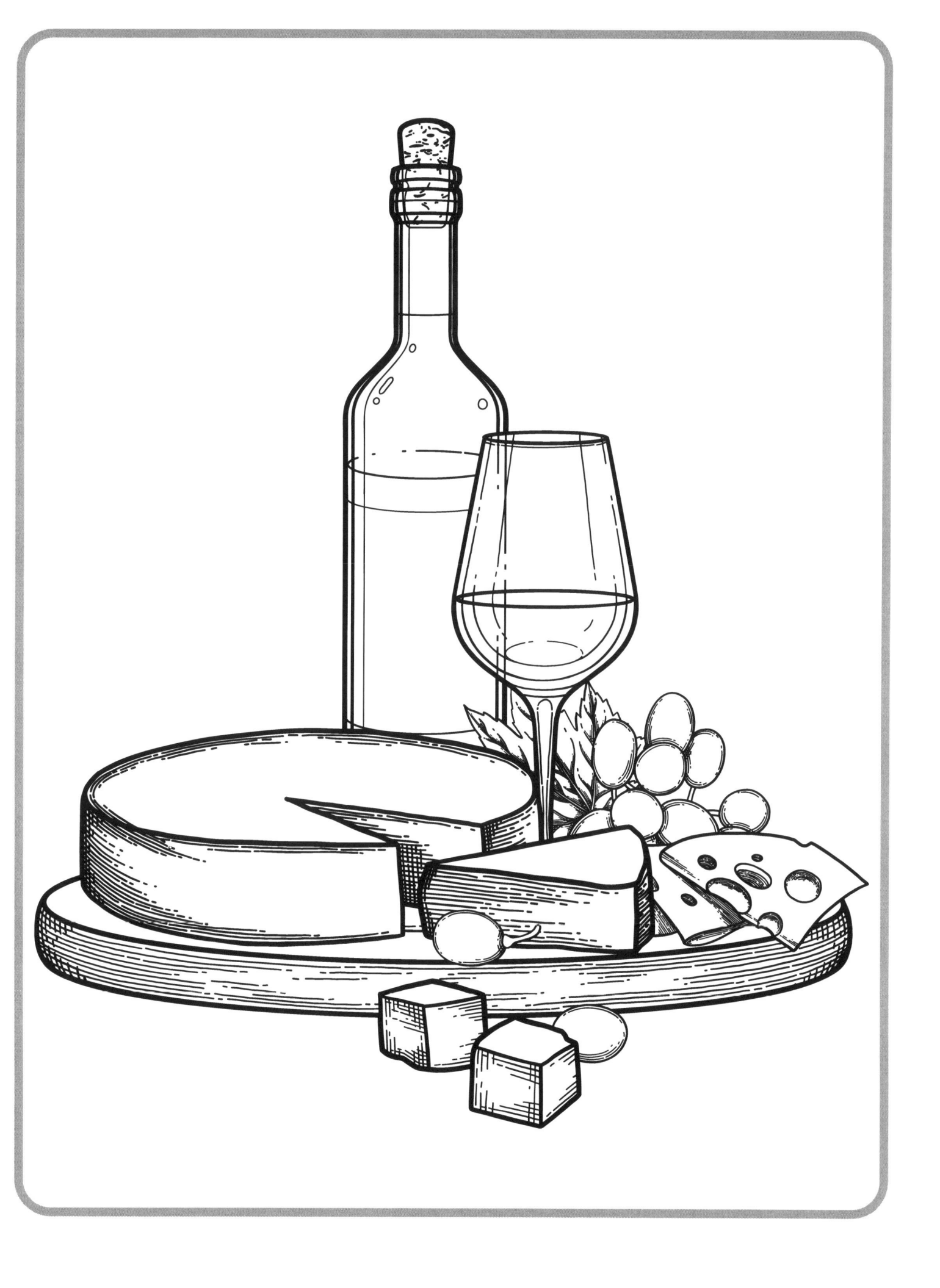

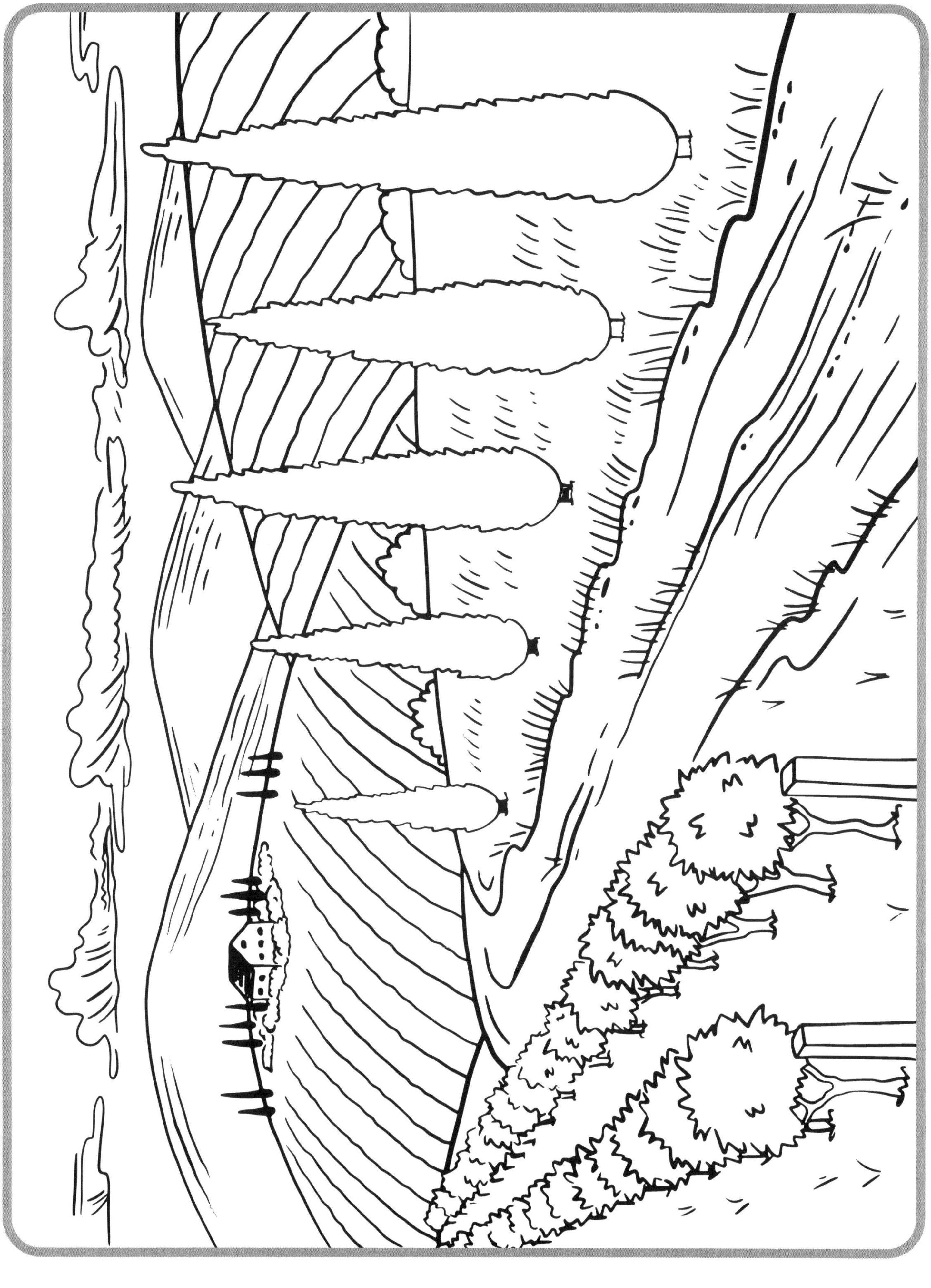

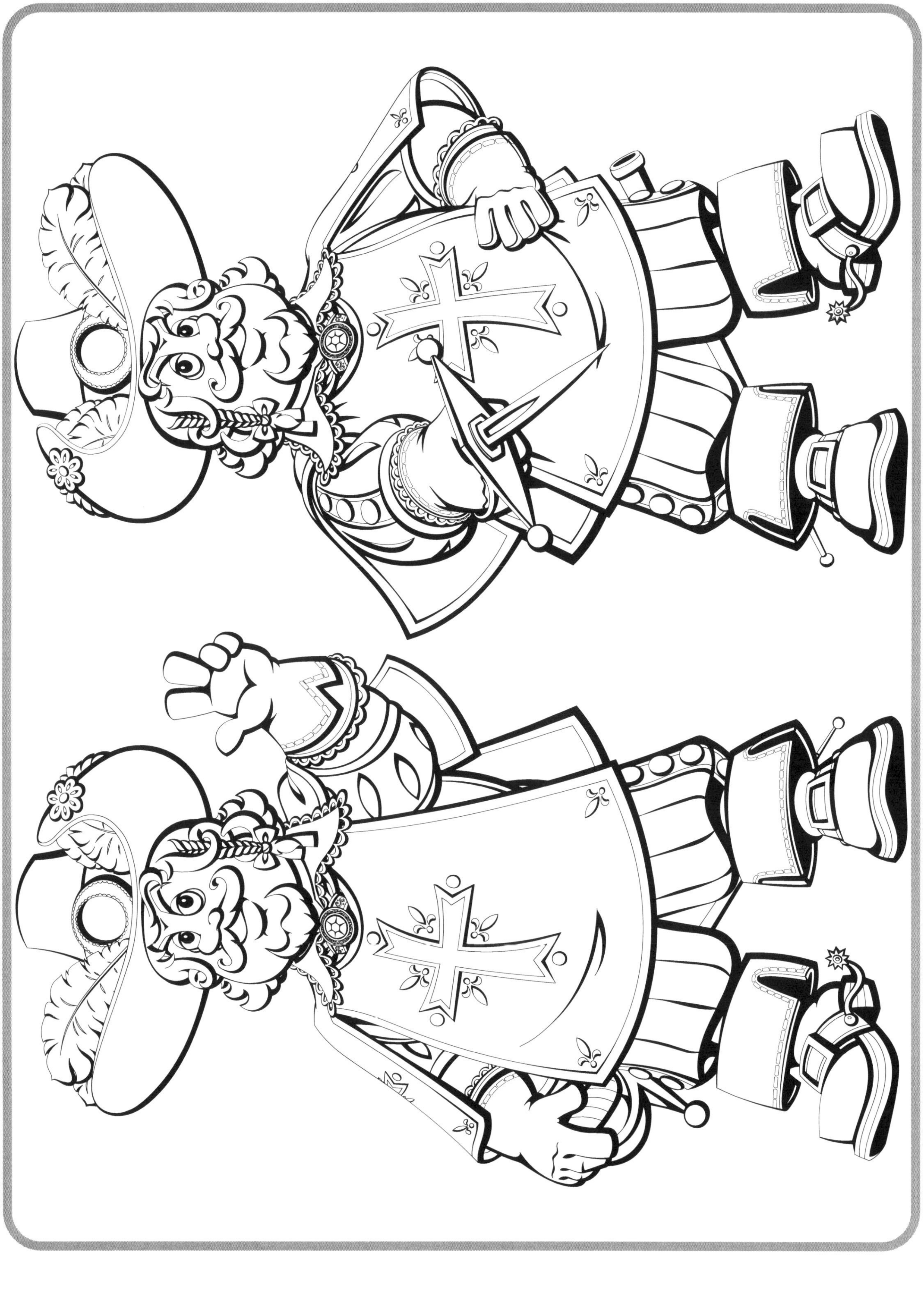

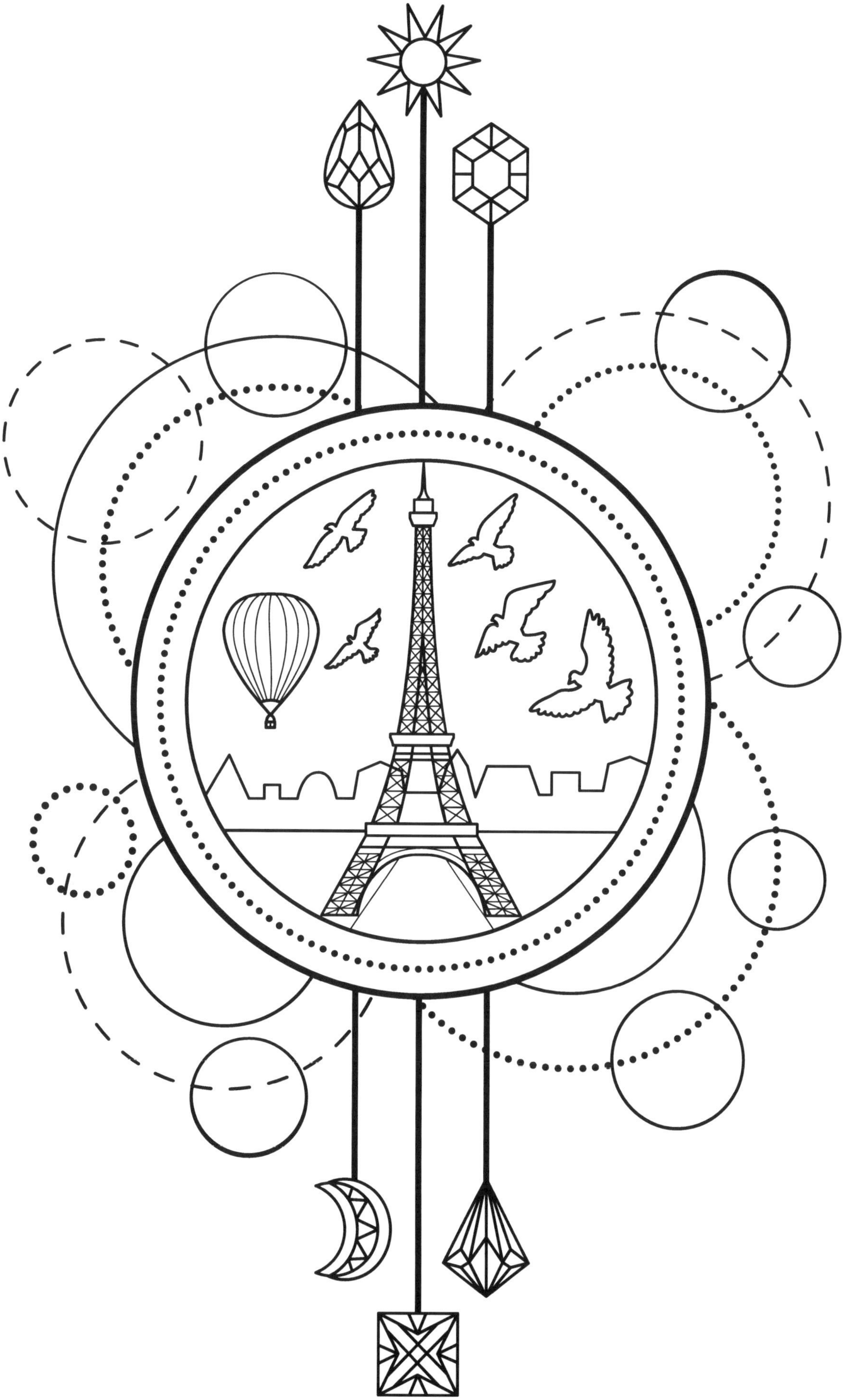

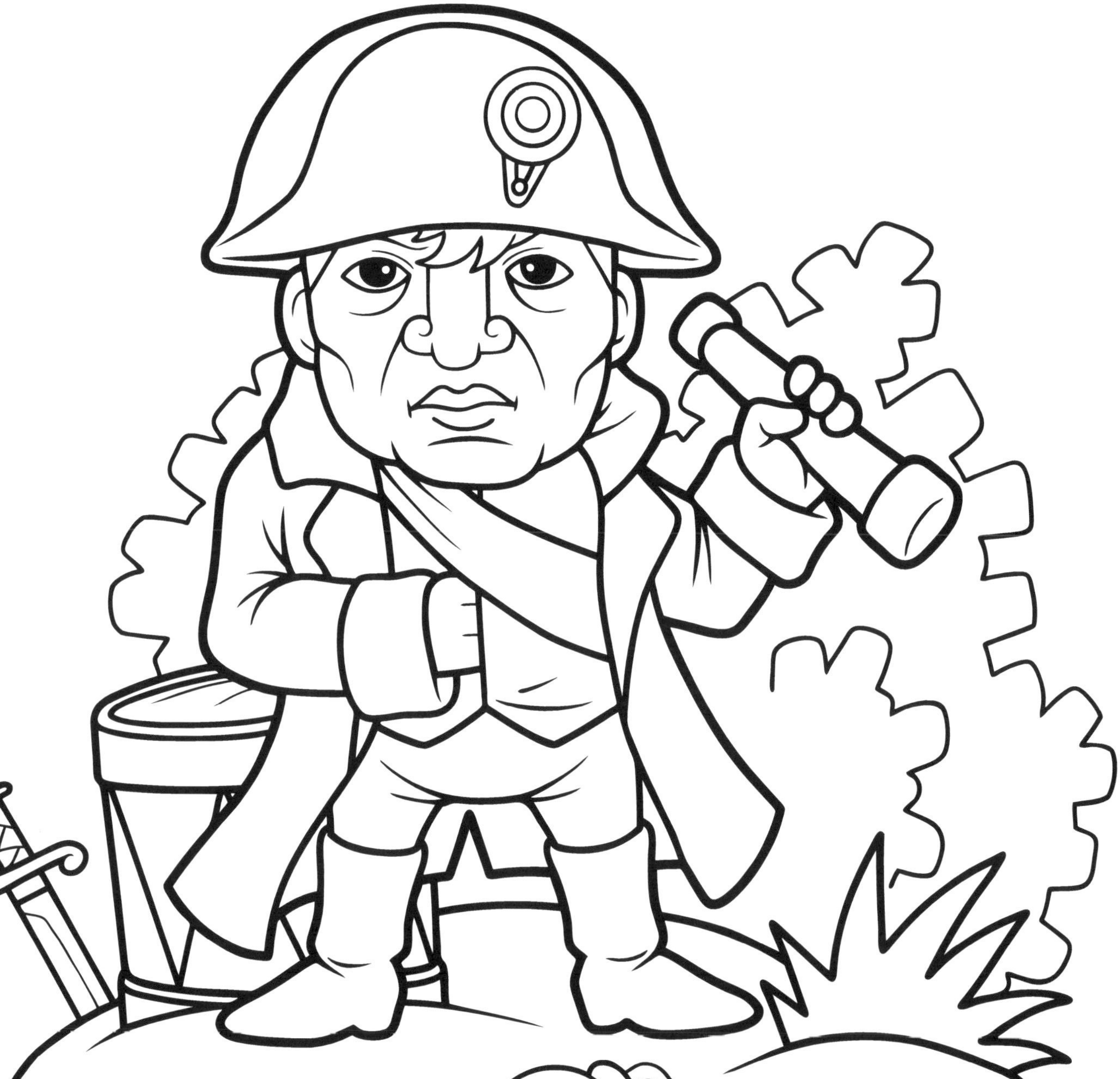

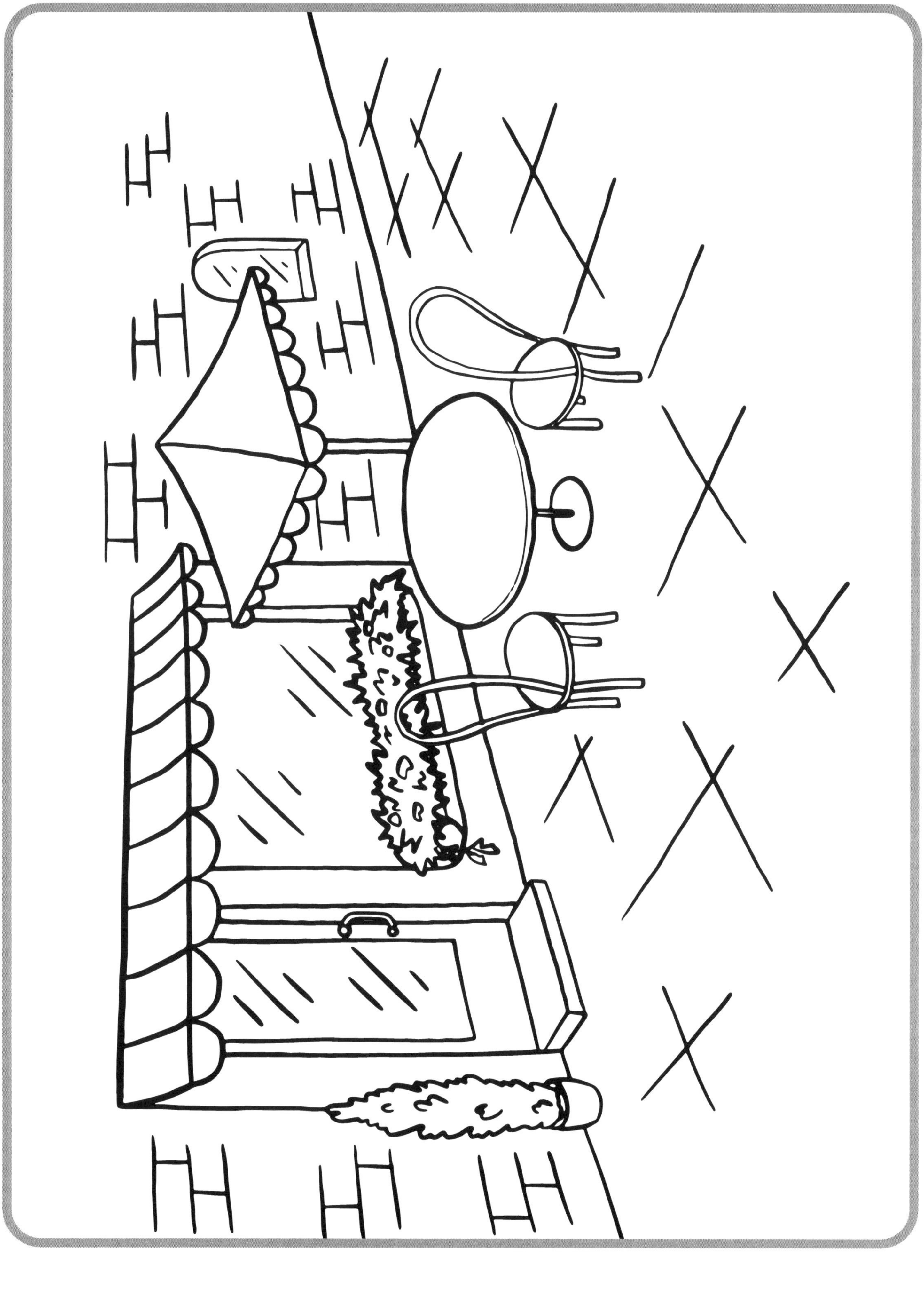

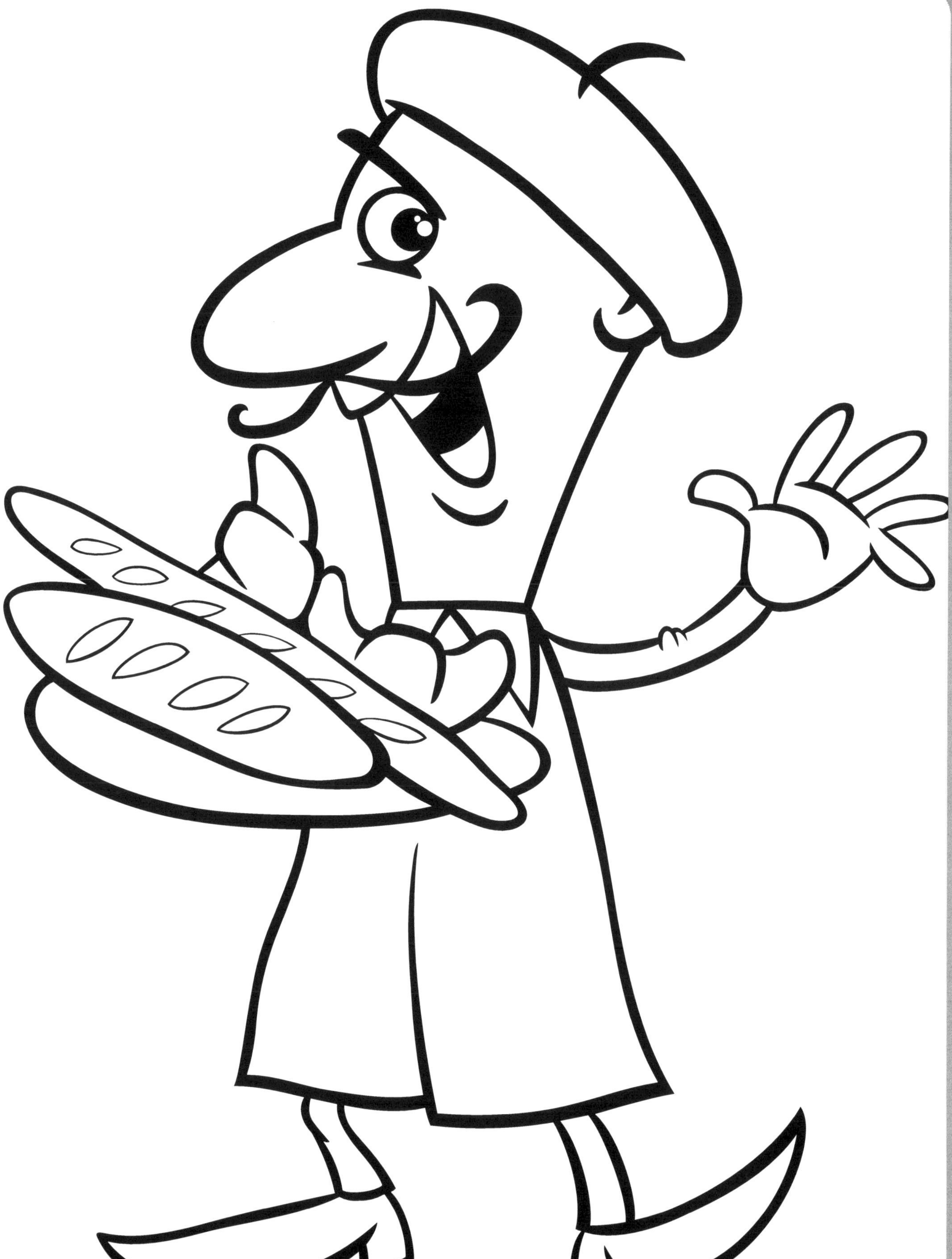

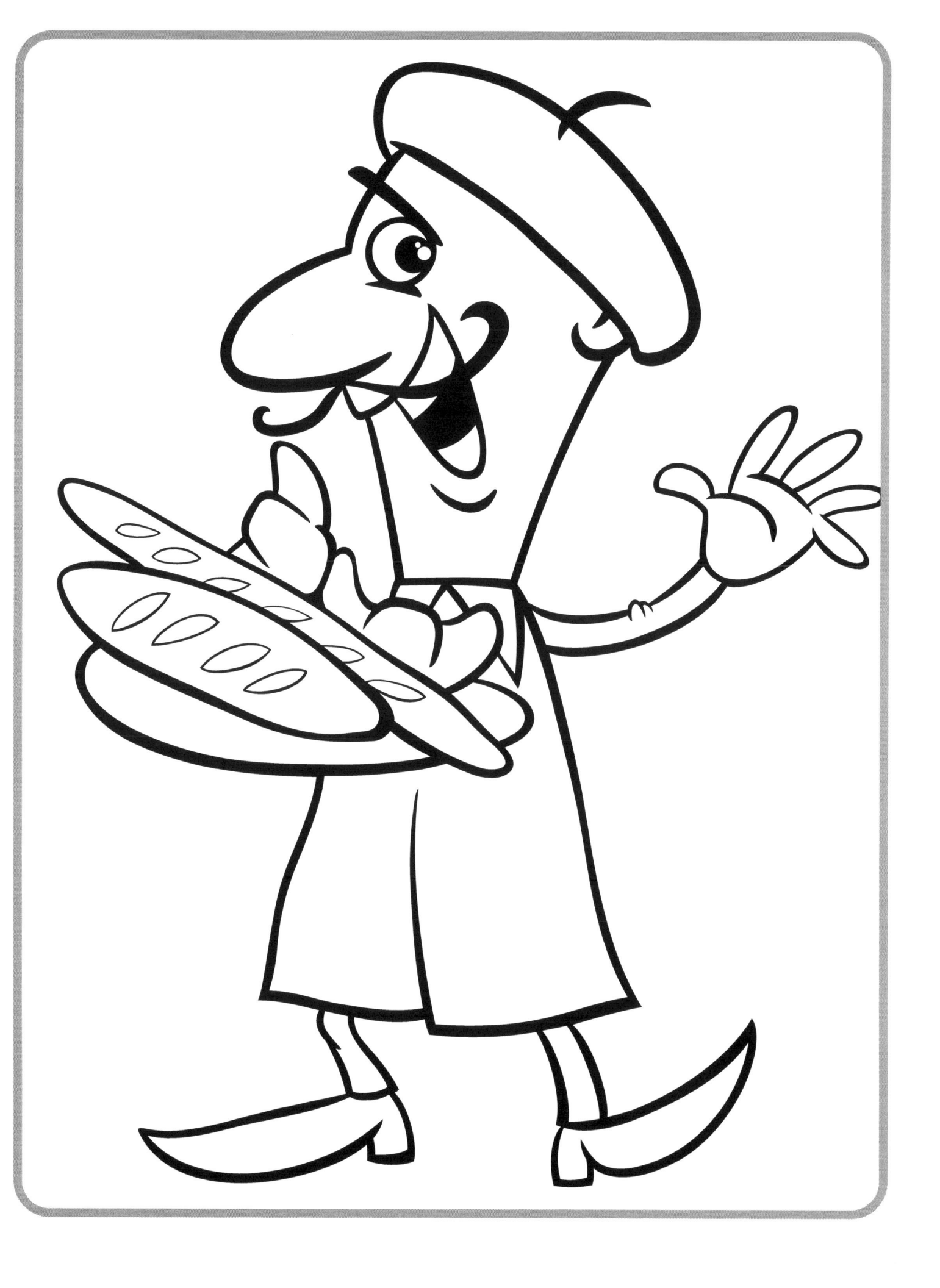

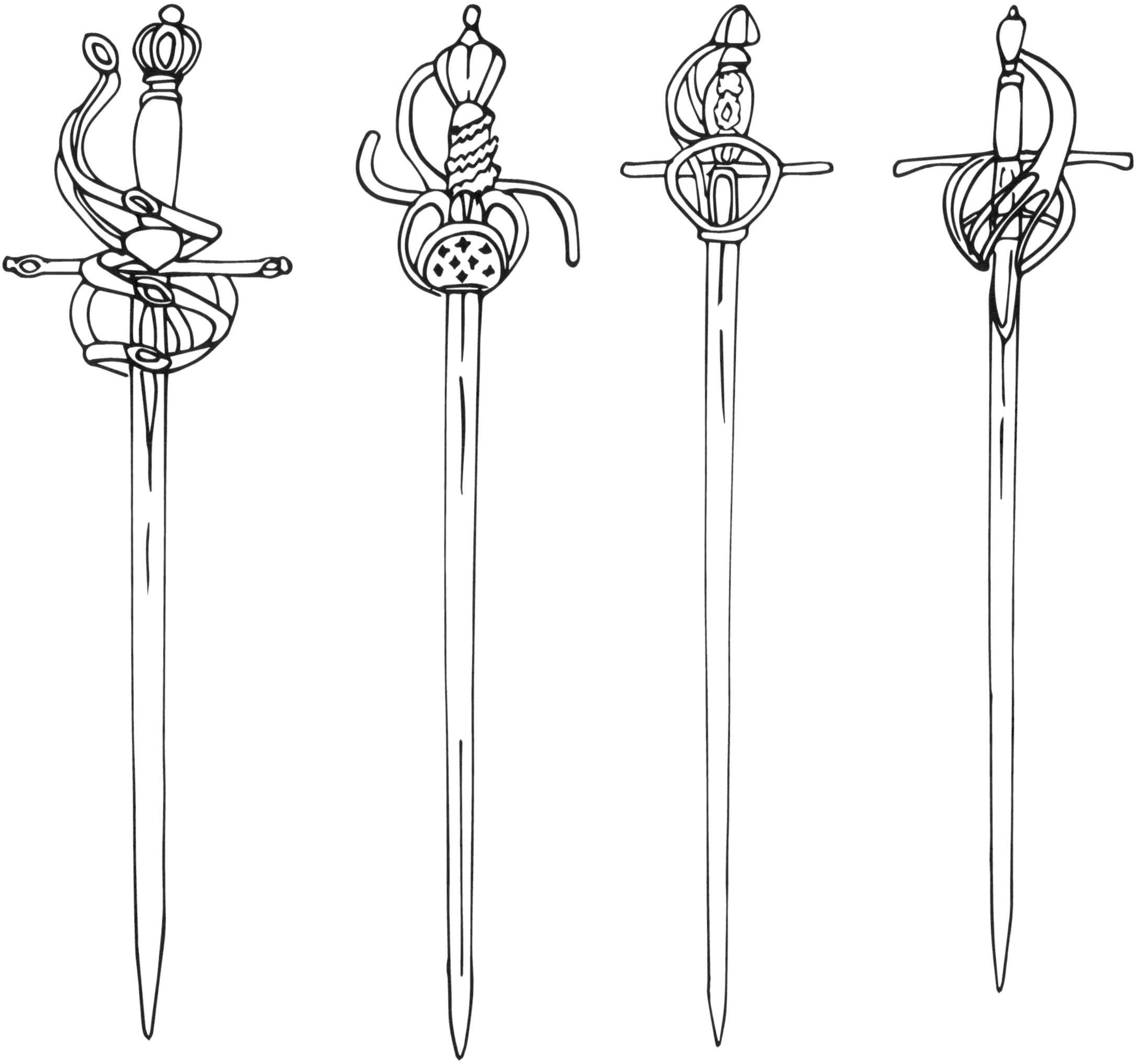

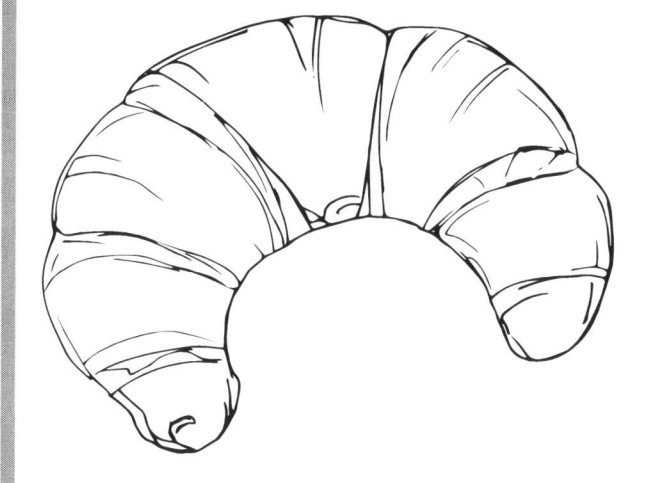

Croissants
for
tea and coffee

french pastries

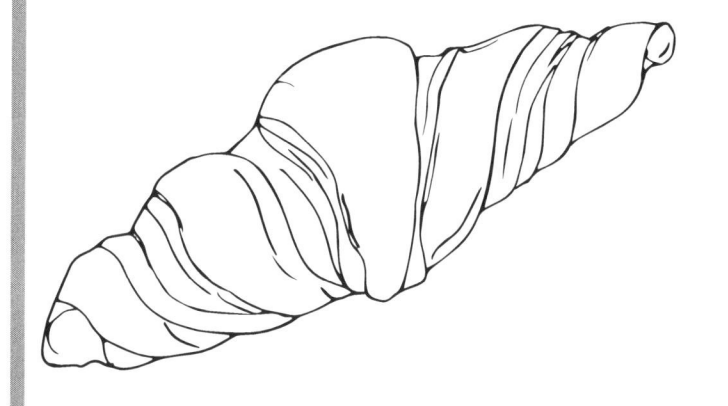

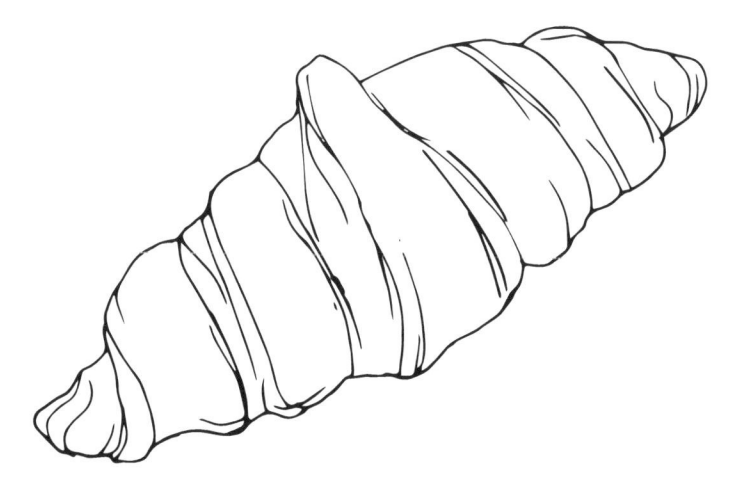

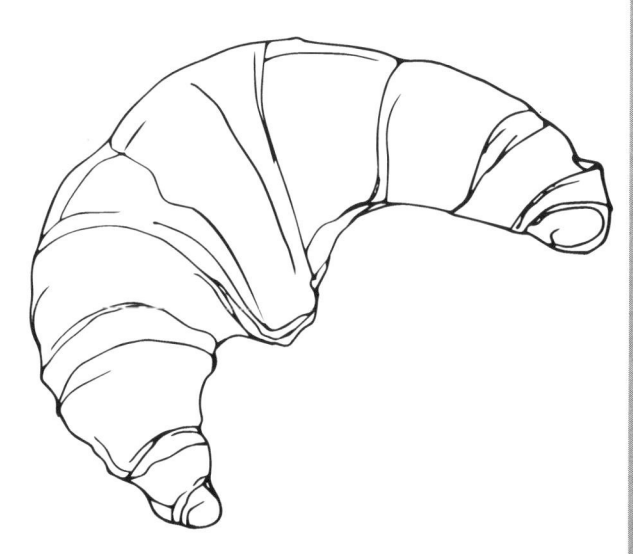

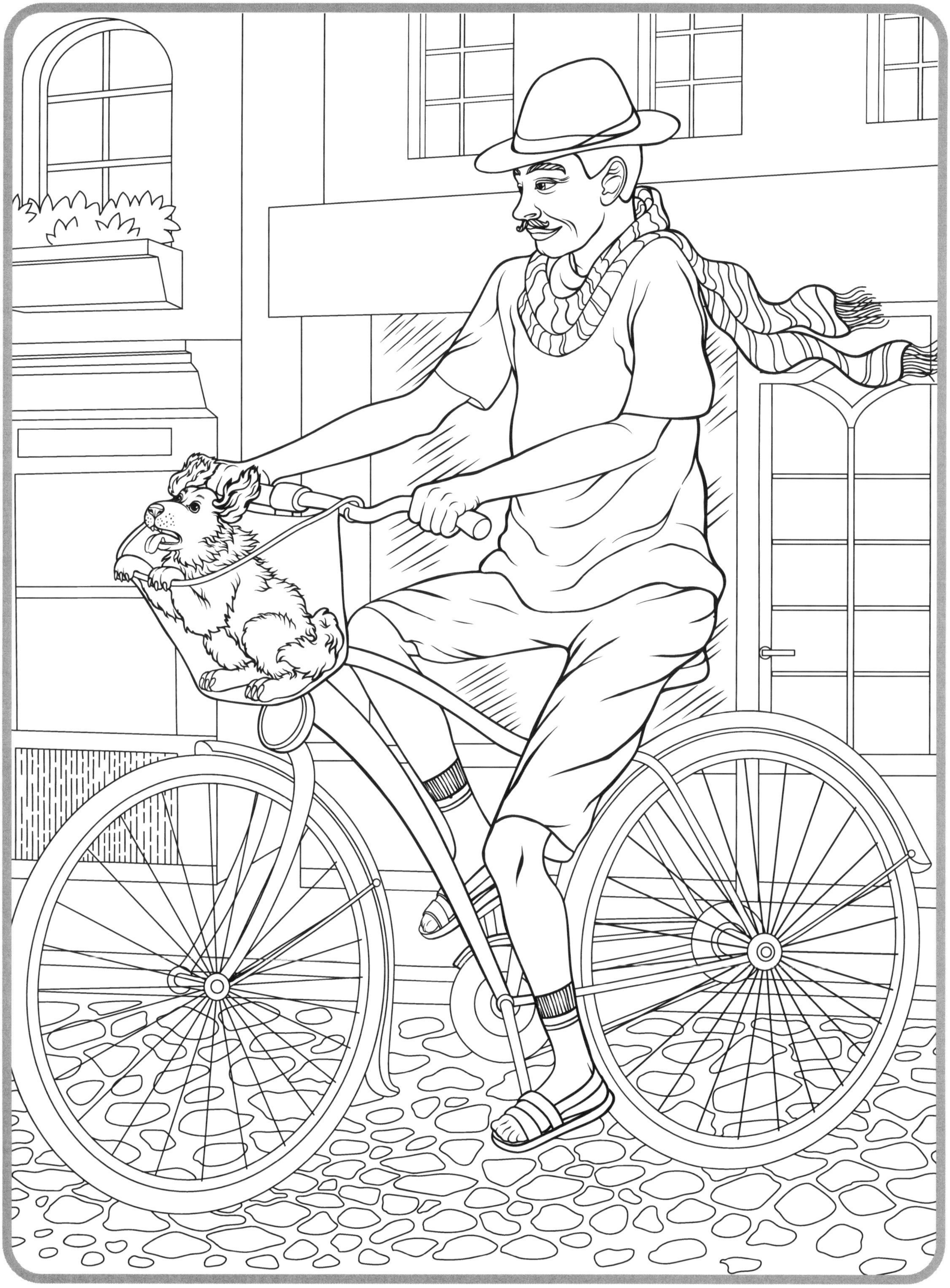

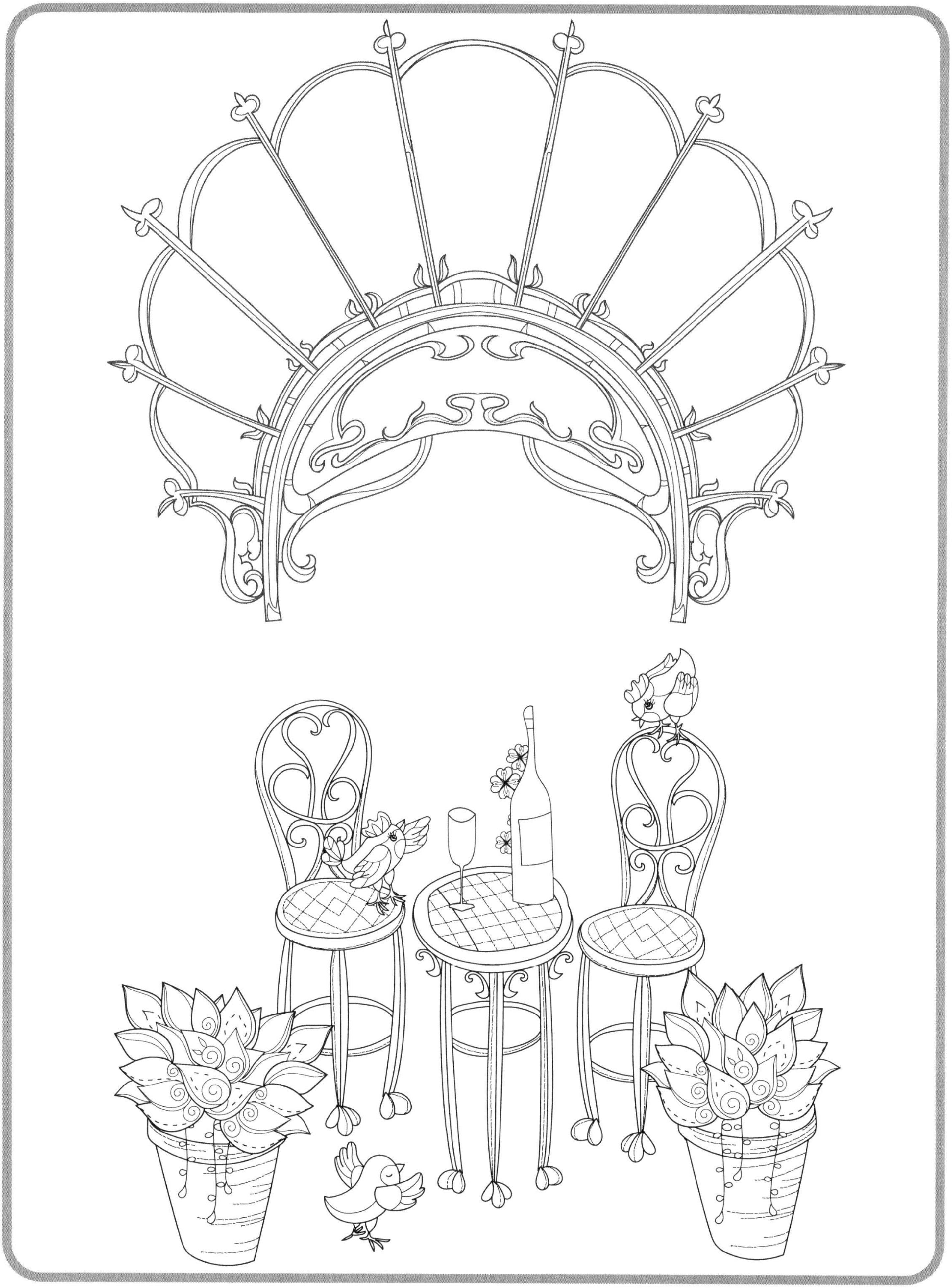

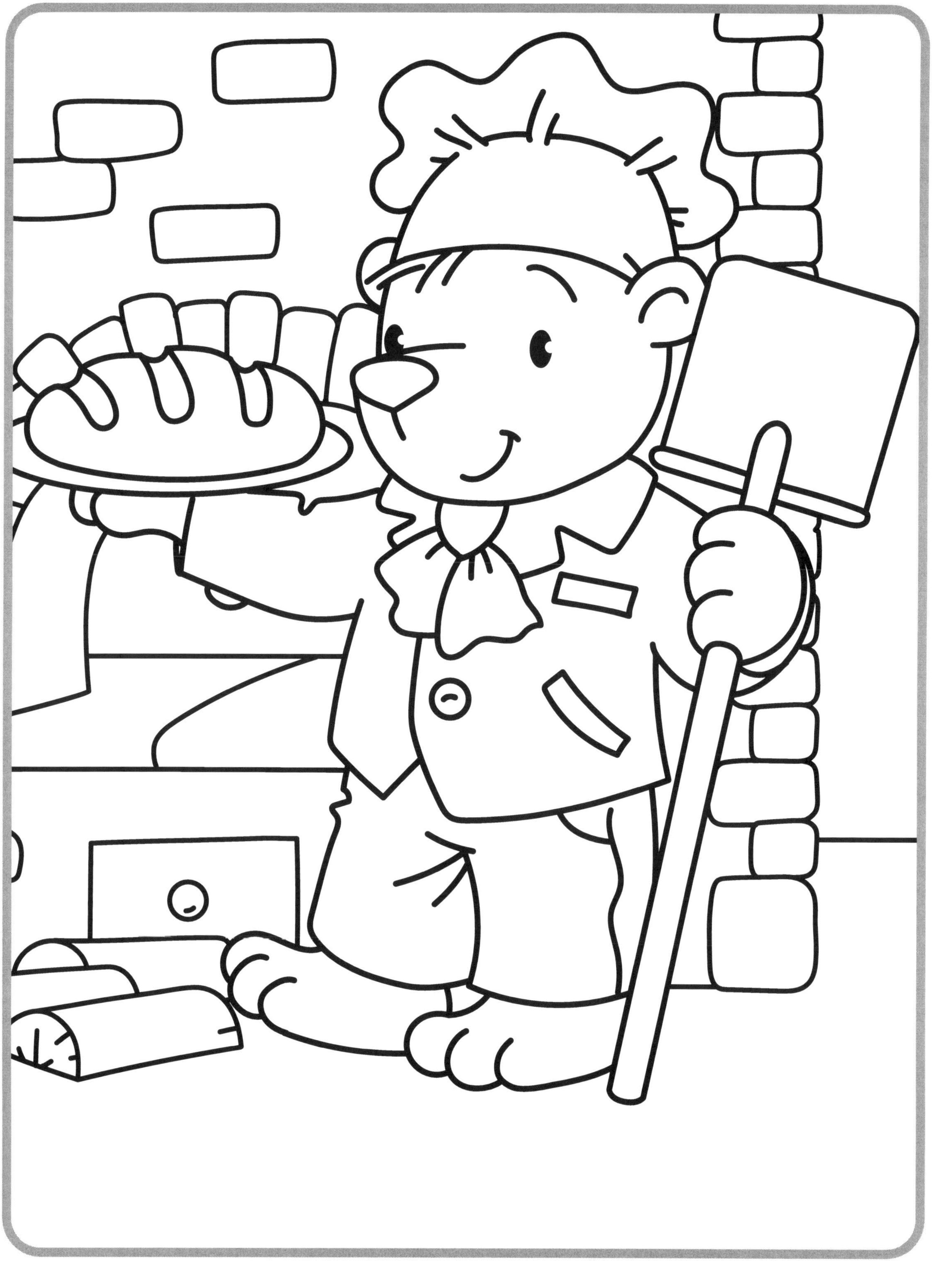

POODLE

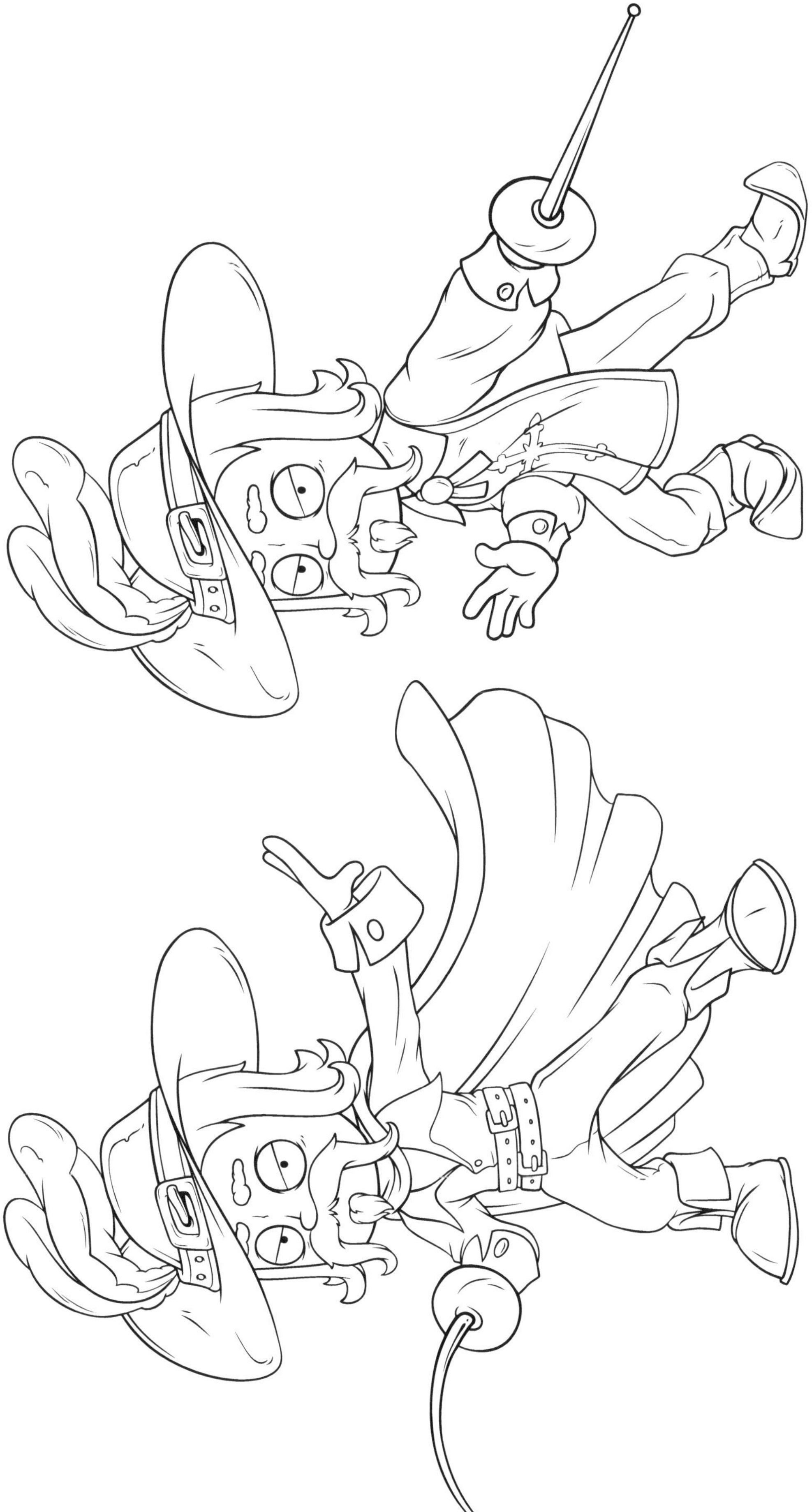

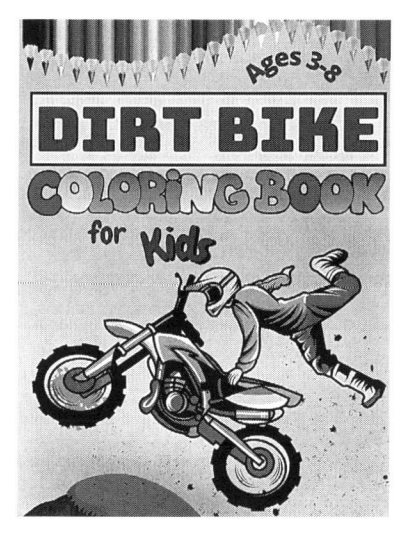

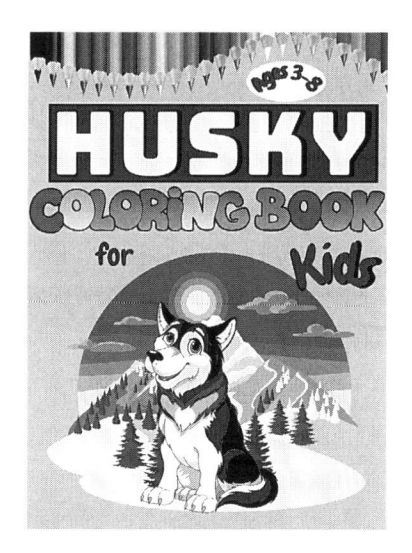

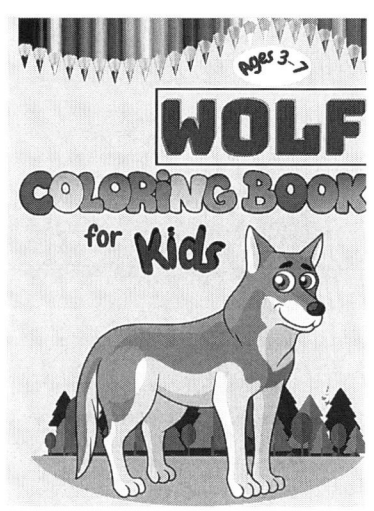

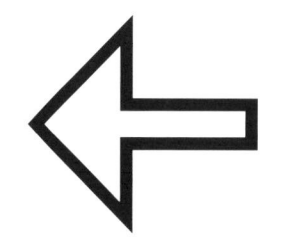

FOR MORE BOOKS SCAN THE QR CODE

Thank you!

inkHORSE Publishing

Printed in Great Britain
by Amazon